More Exciting Easy Classics

For Piano

Arranged by Charles Bateman

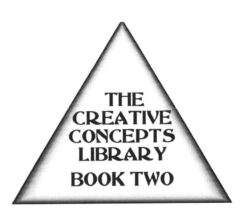

THE CREATIVE CONCEPTS LIBRARY BOOK TWO

Catalog #07-2054

ISBN# 1-56922-162-6

Printed in the United States of America
Produced by John L. Haag
Cover Painting by Mary Woodin ~ London, England

Exclusive Distributor:
CREATIVE CONCEPTS PUBLISHING CORPORATION
2290 Eastman Avenue #110, Ventura, California 93003
Check out our Web site at *http://www.creativeconcepts.com* or you can Email us at *mail@creativeconcepts.com*

CONTENTS

CONTENTS

4

AIR FOR THE G STRING

Johann Sebastian Bach

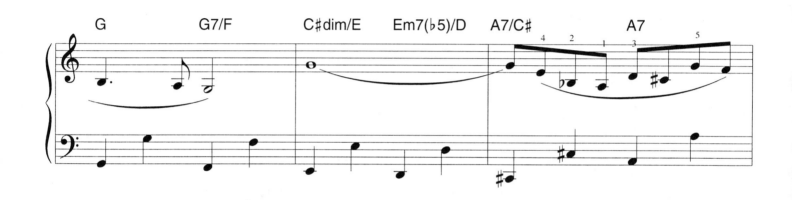

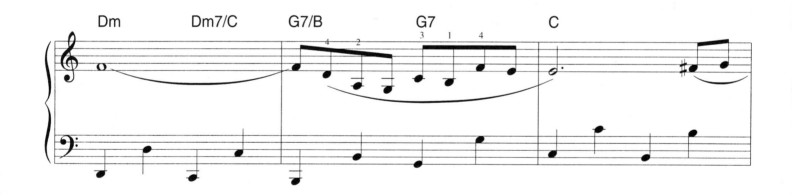

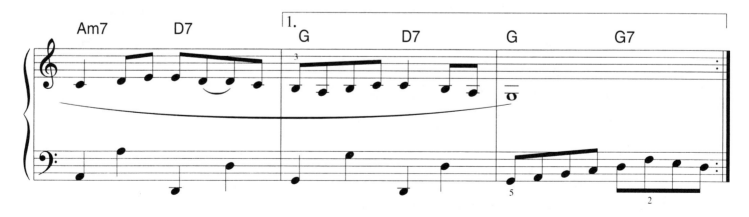

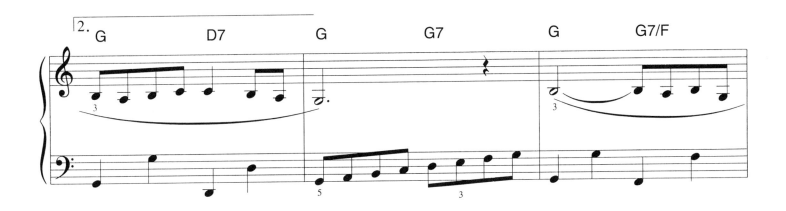

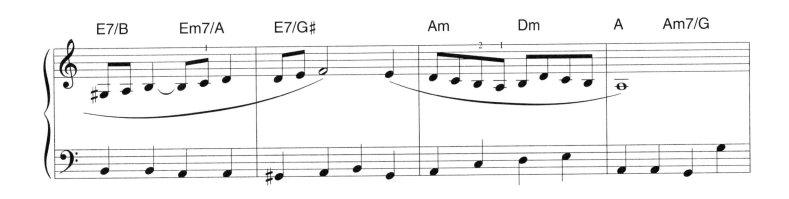

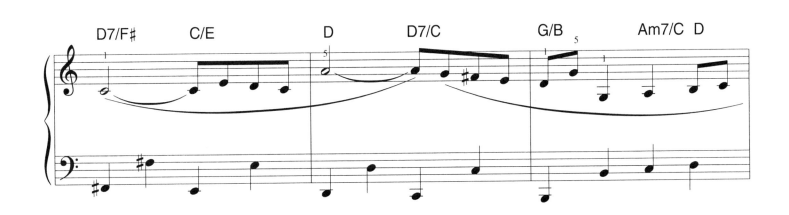

6

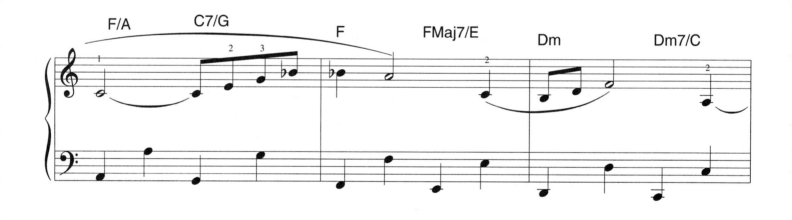

AUSTRIAN HYMN

Joseph Haydn

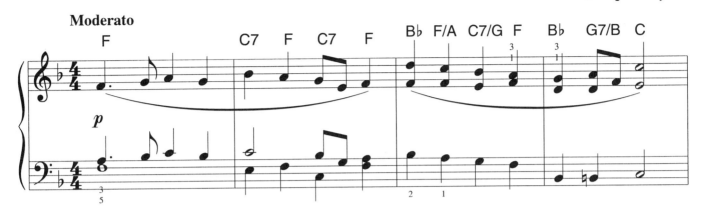

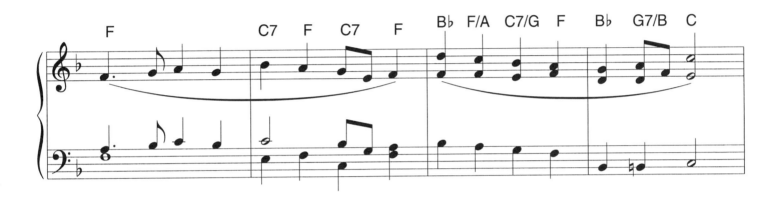

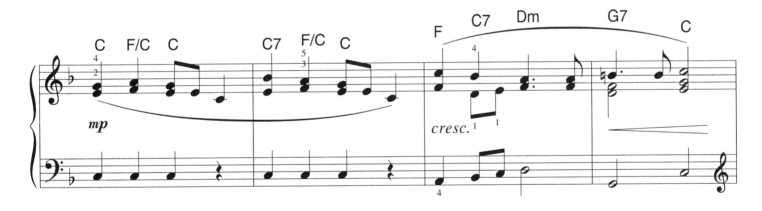

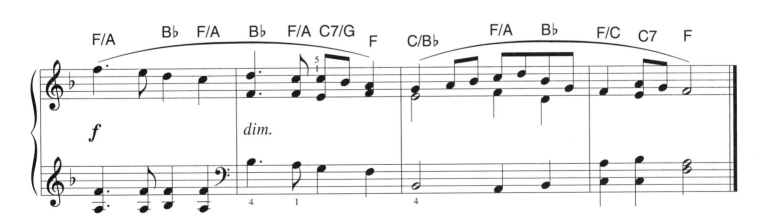

BARCAROLLE
(from "Tales of Hoffman")

Moderato

Jacques Offenbach

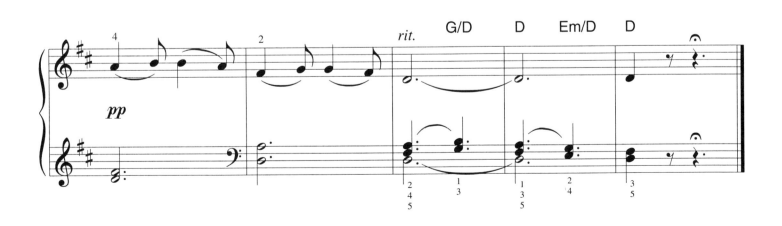

THE BIRDCATCHER'S SONG
(FROM THE MAGIC FLUTE)

Wolfgang Amadeus Mozart

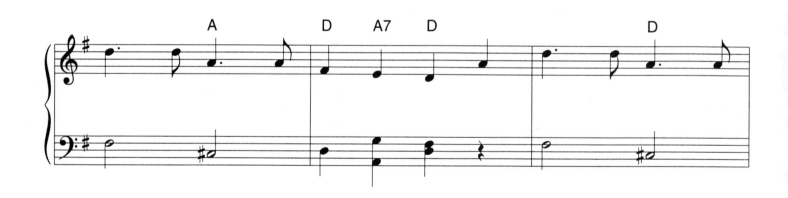

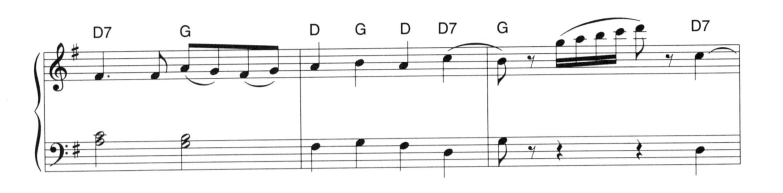

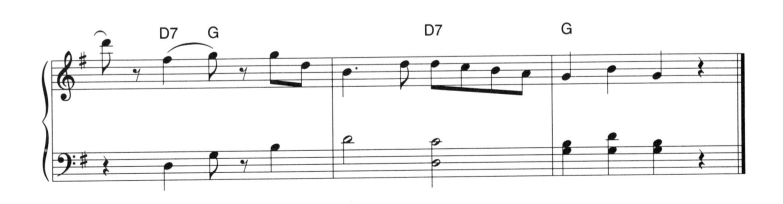

BROTHERLY LOVE

Ludwig van Beethoven

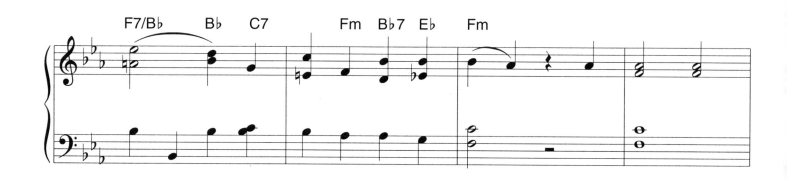

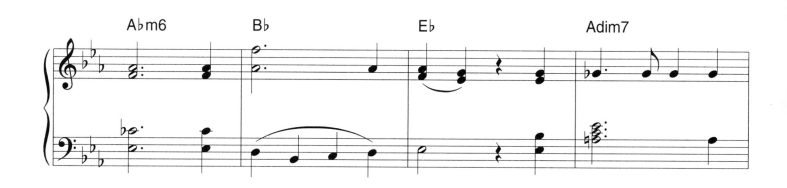

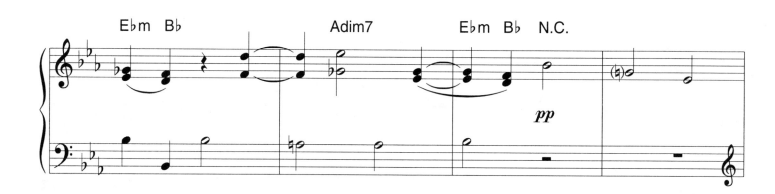

CHANSON TRISTE

Pyotr Ilyich Tchaikovsky

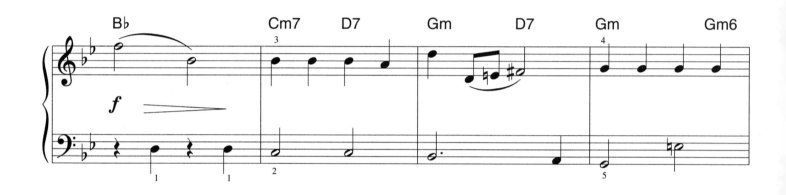

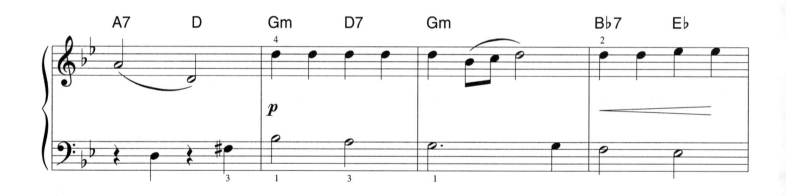

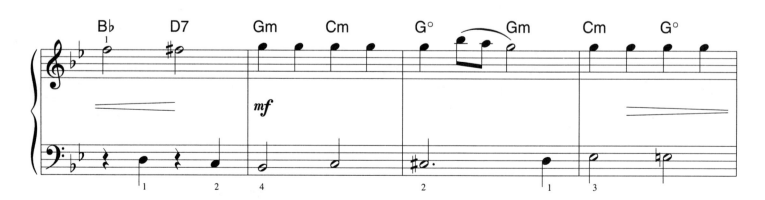

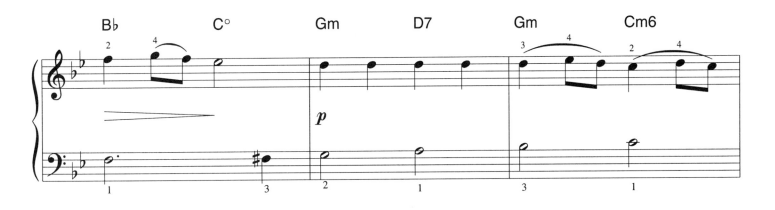

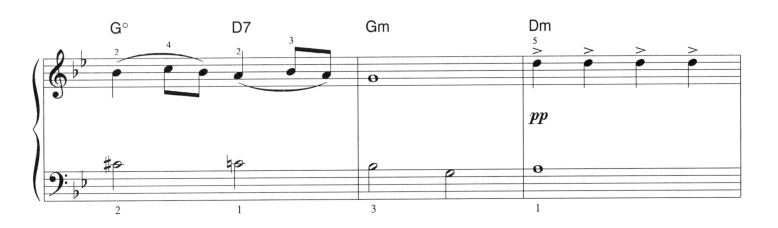

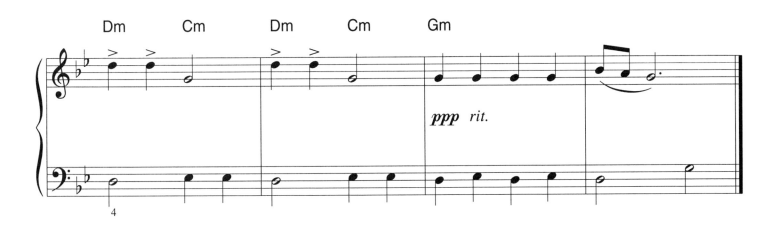

CHILDREN'S CARNIVAL

Louis Streabbog

Fine

D.C. al Fine

THE CRICKET AND THE BUMBLE BEE

George Chadwick

21

CIRIBIRIBIN

A. Pestalozza

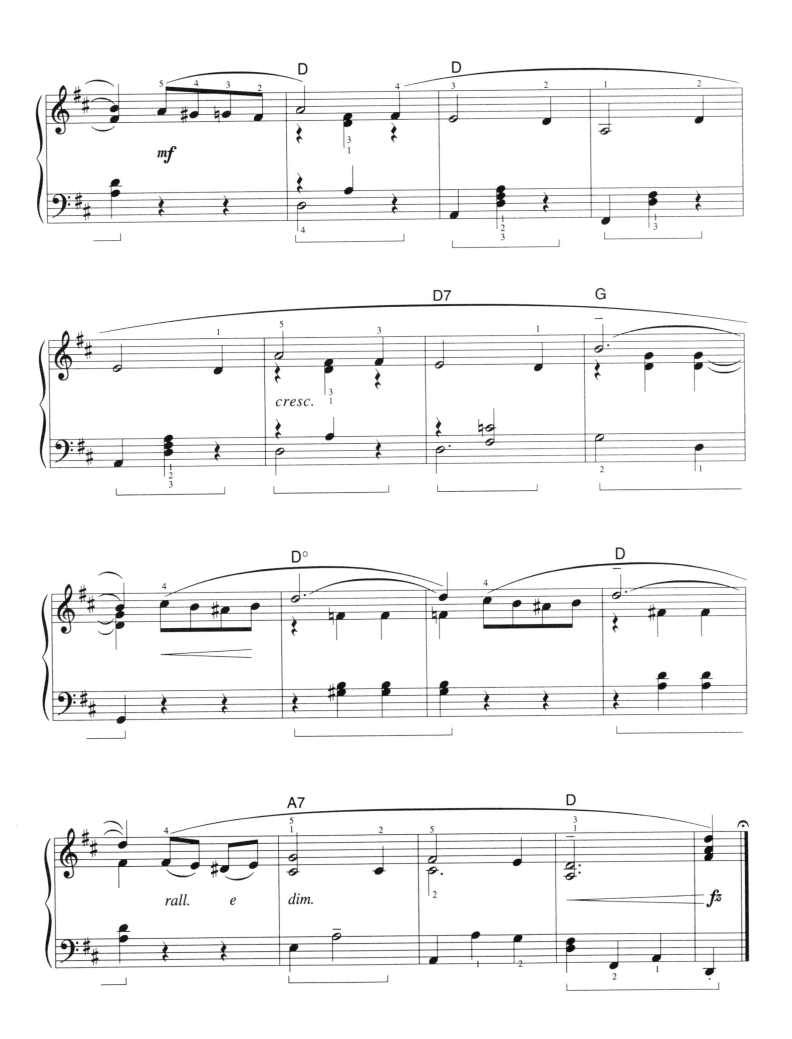

Theme from
DEATH AND THE MAIDEN

Franz Schubert

THE FAIR

Cornelius Gurlitt

Vivace (lively)

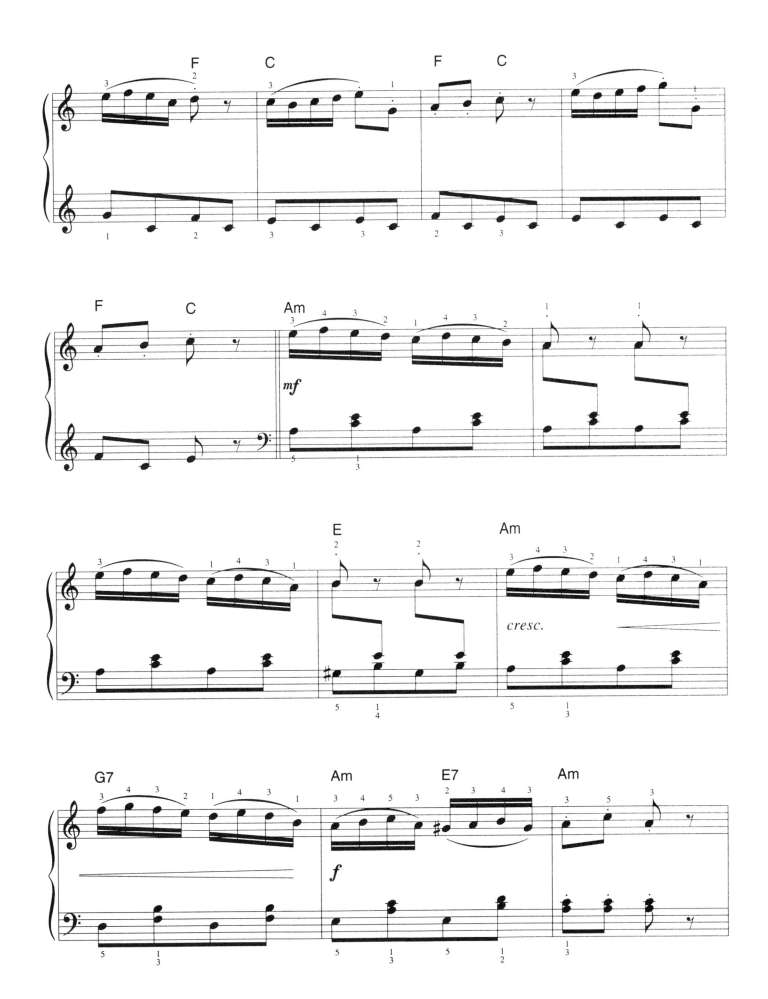

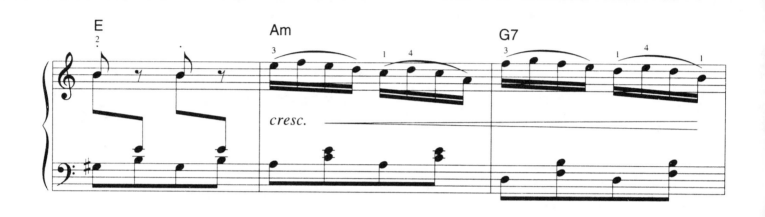

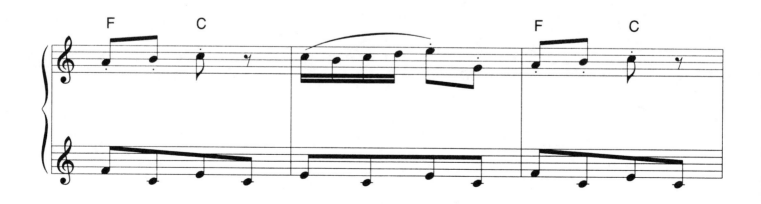

Theme from
FINALE OF SYMPHONY NO. 1

Gustav Mahler

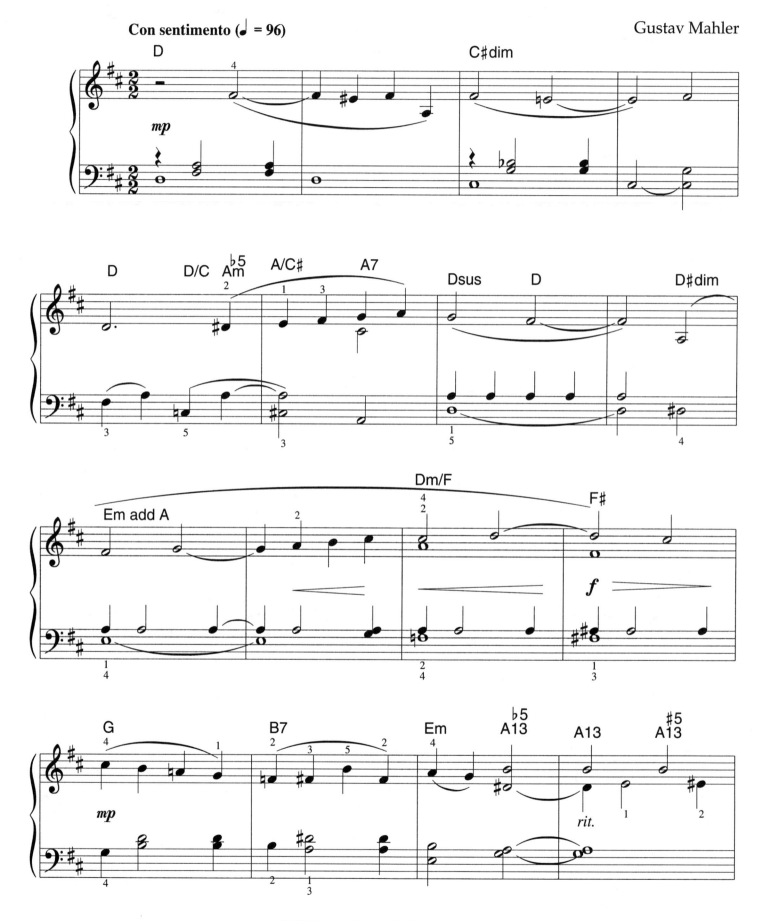

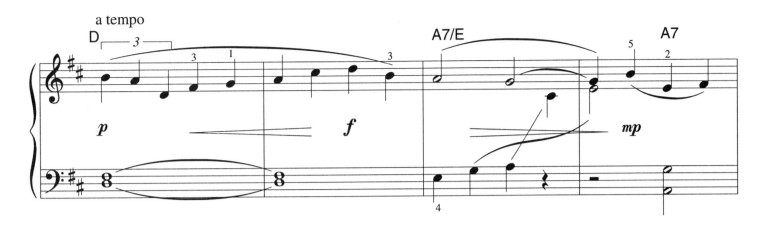

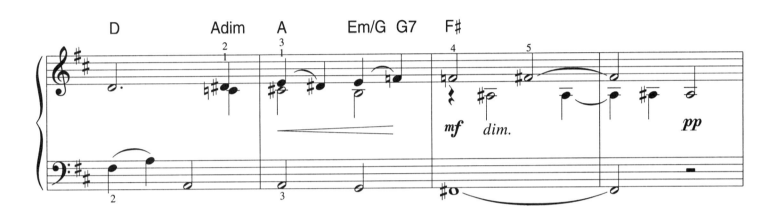

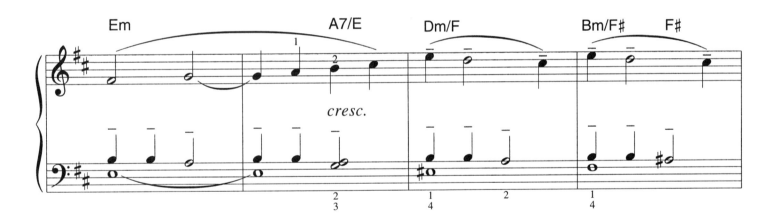

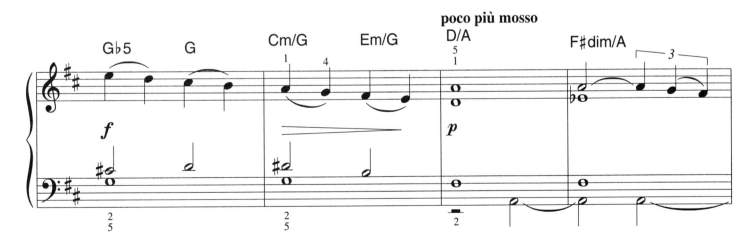

32

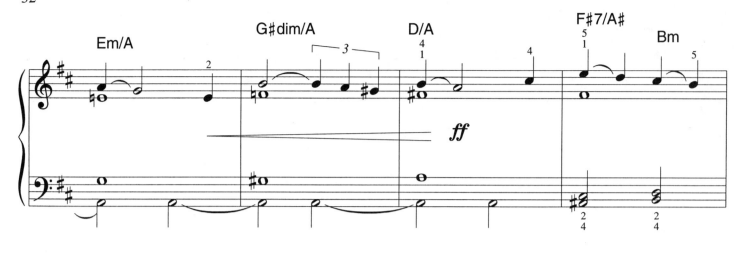

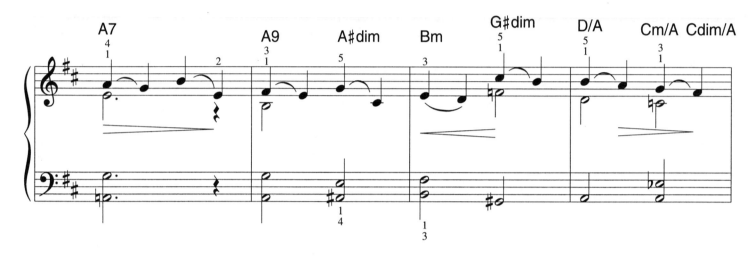

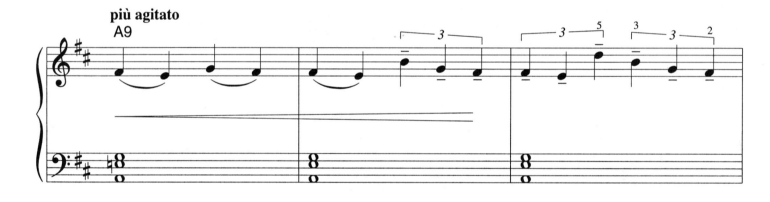

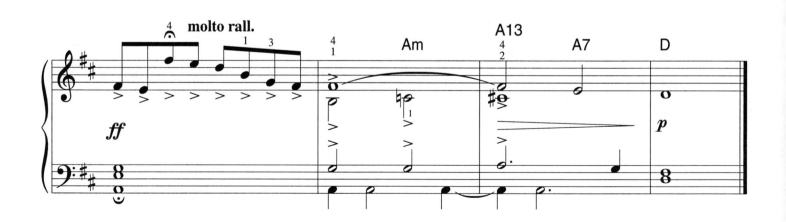

THE GALLOPING COMEDIANS

Dmitri Kabalevsky

Fine

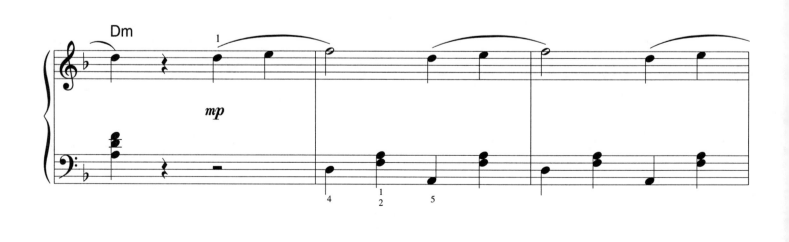

D. C. al Fine

FLIGHT OF THE ROBIN

German Melody

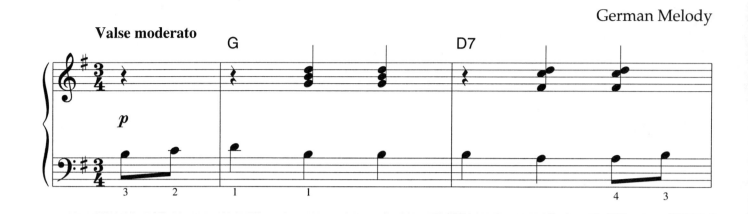

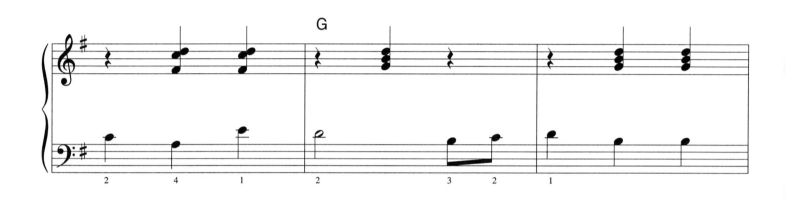

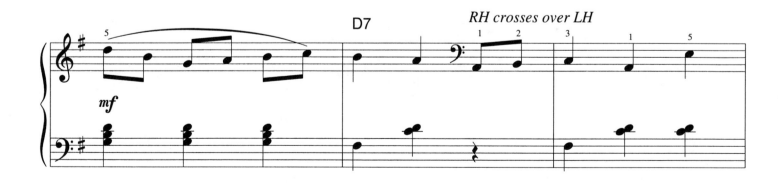

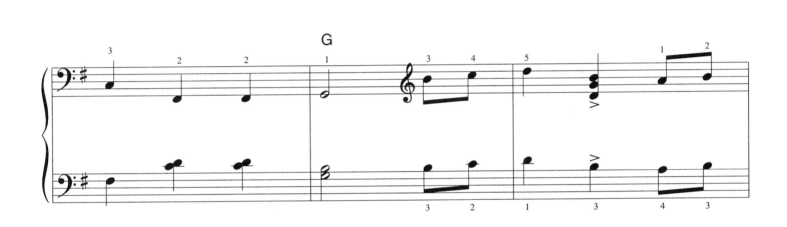

HUMORESQUE
(Opus 101, No. 7)

Anton Dvorak

Fine

D.C. al Fine

LITTLE PRINCESS WALTZ

Franz Josef Haydn

IN MAY

Franz Behr

JESU, JOY OF MAN'S DESIRING

Johann Sebastian Bach

Slowly and evenly

THE LITTLE SHEPHERD
(from "The Children's Corner")

Claude Debussy

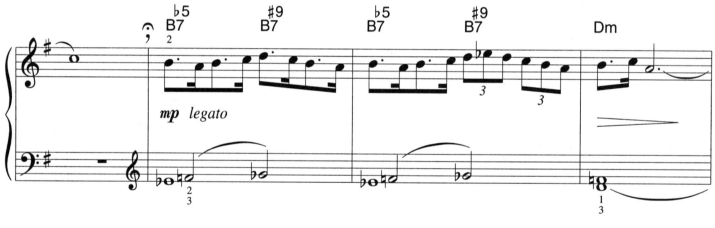

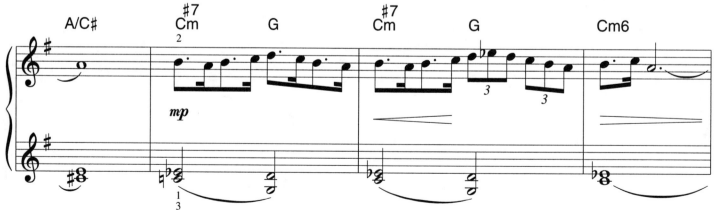

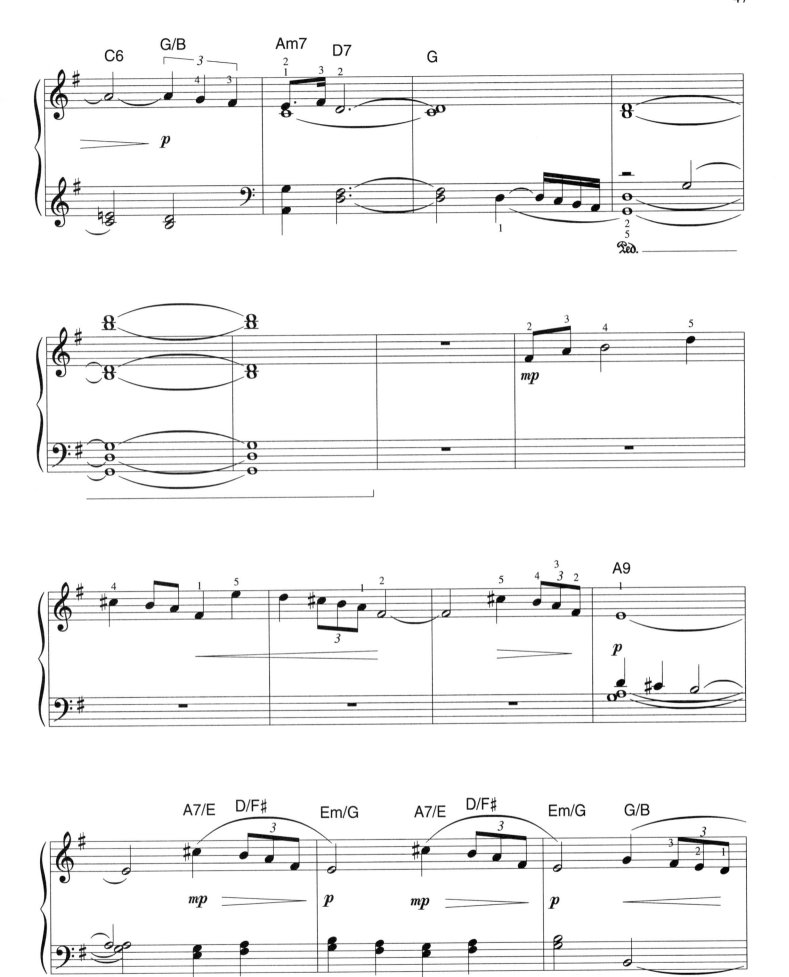

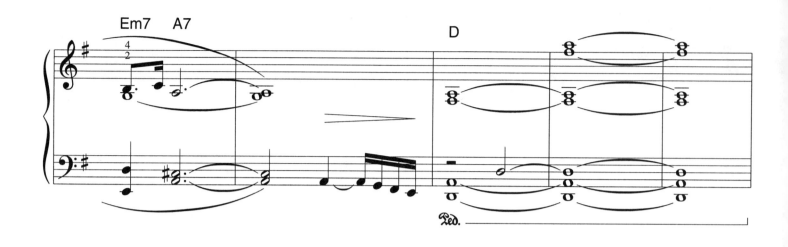

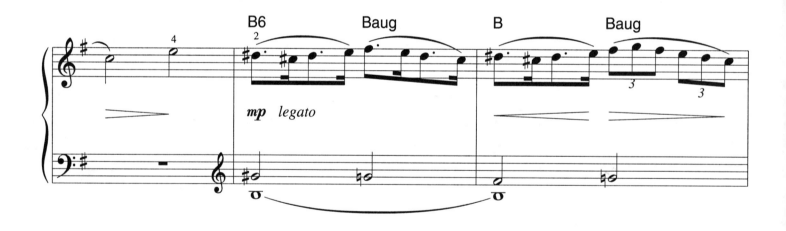

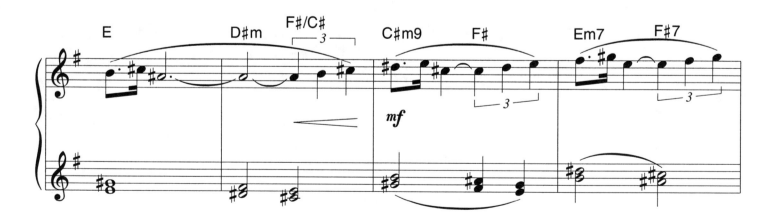

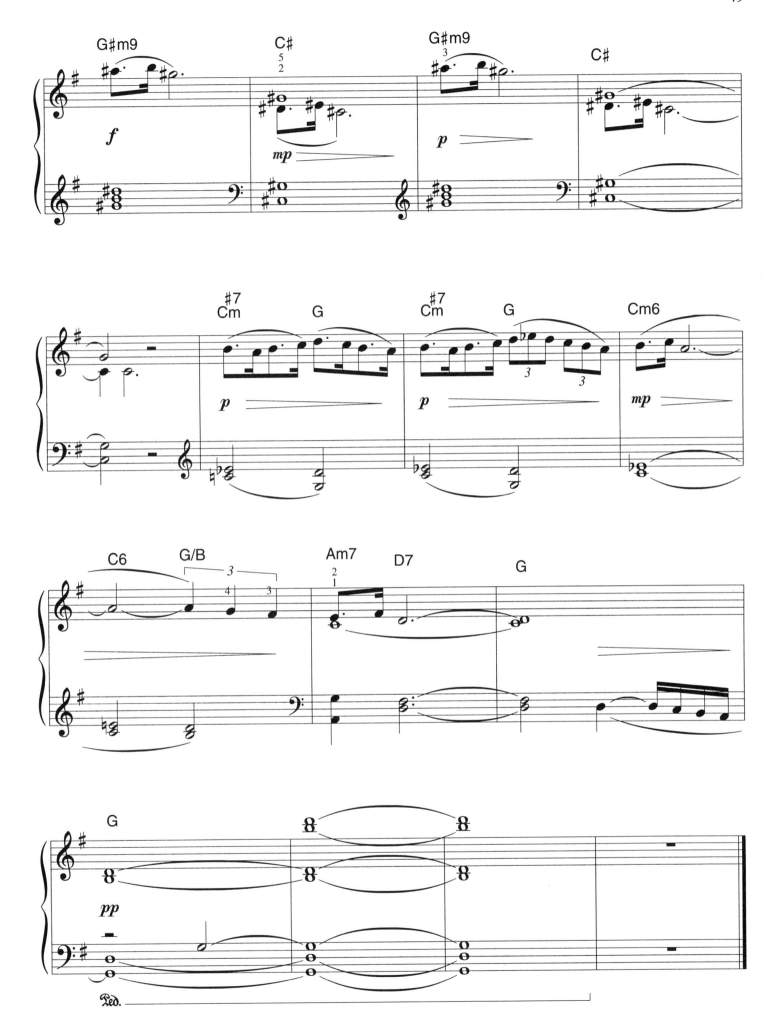

MATTINATA

Freely moving

Ruggiero Leoncavallo

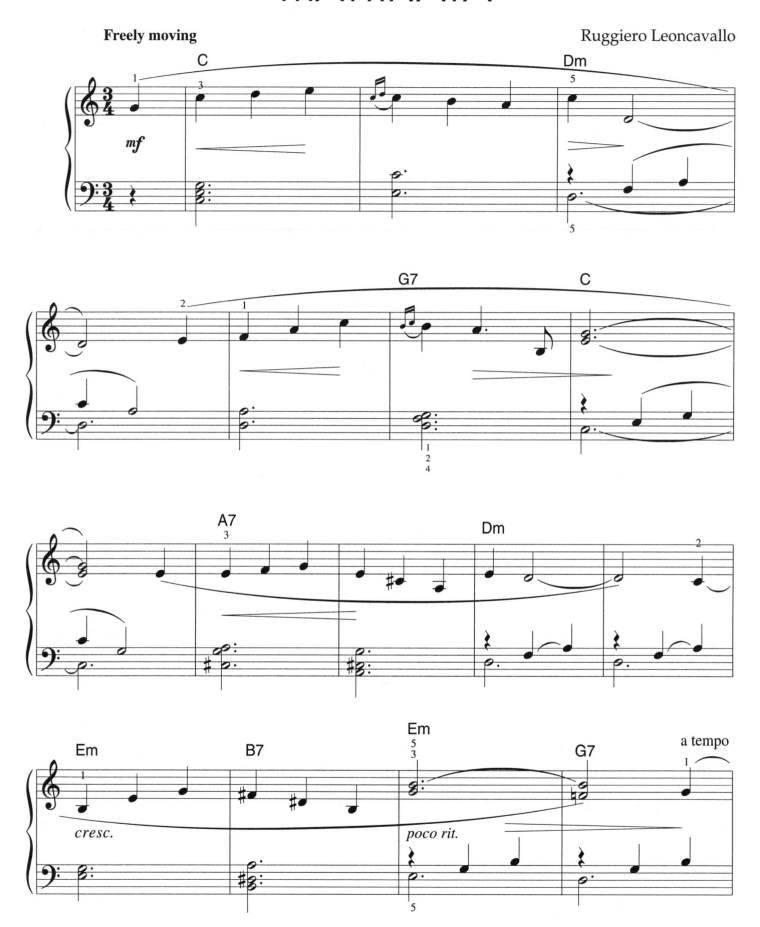

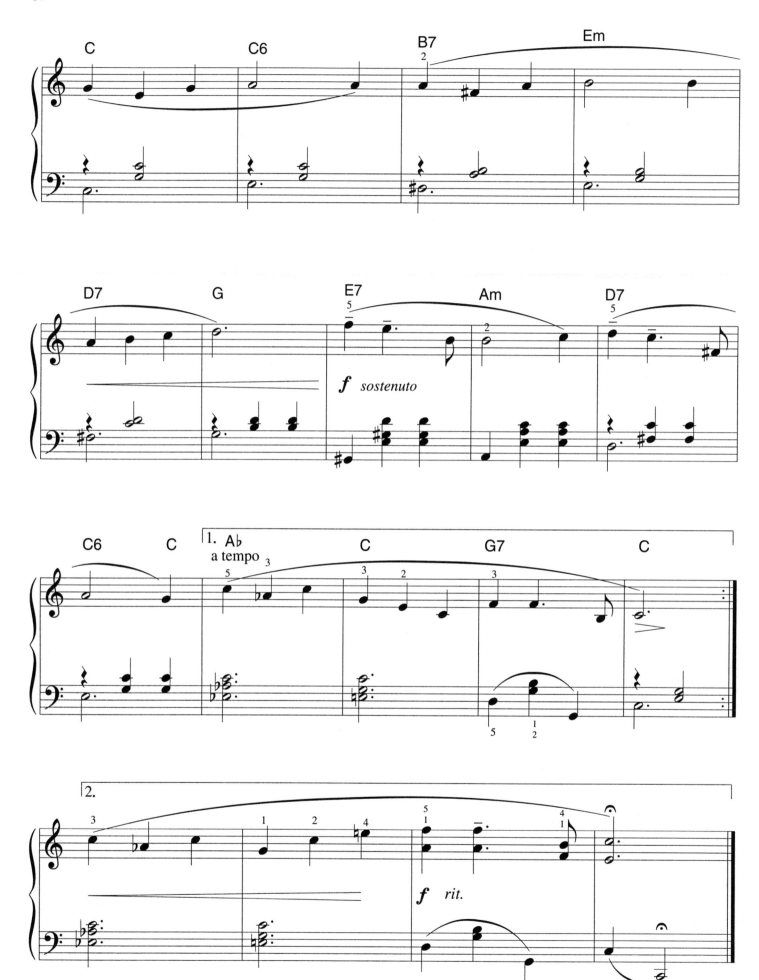

MELODY IN F

Rubinstein

54

MEDITATION
(from "Thaïs")

Jules Massenet

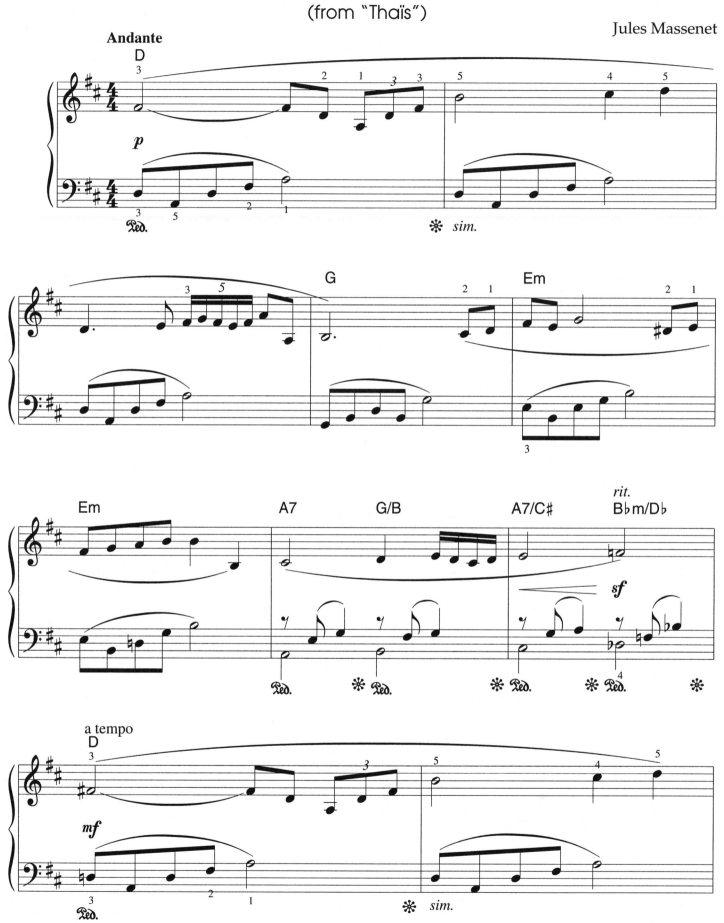

MERRY WIDOW WALTZ

Franz Lehar

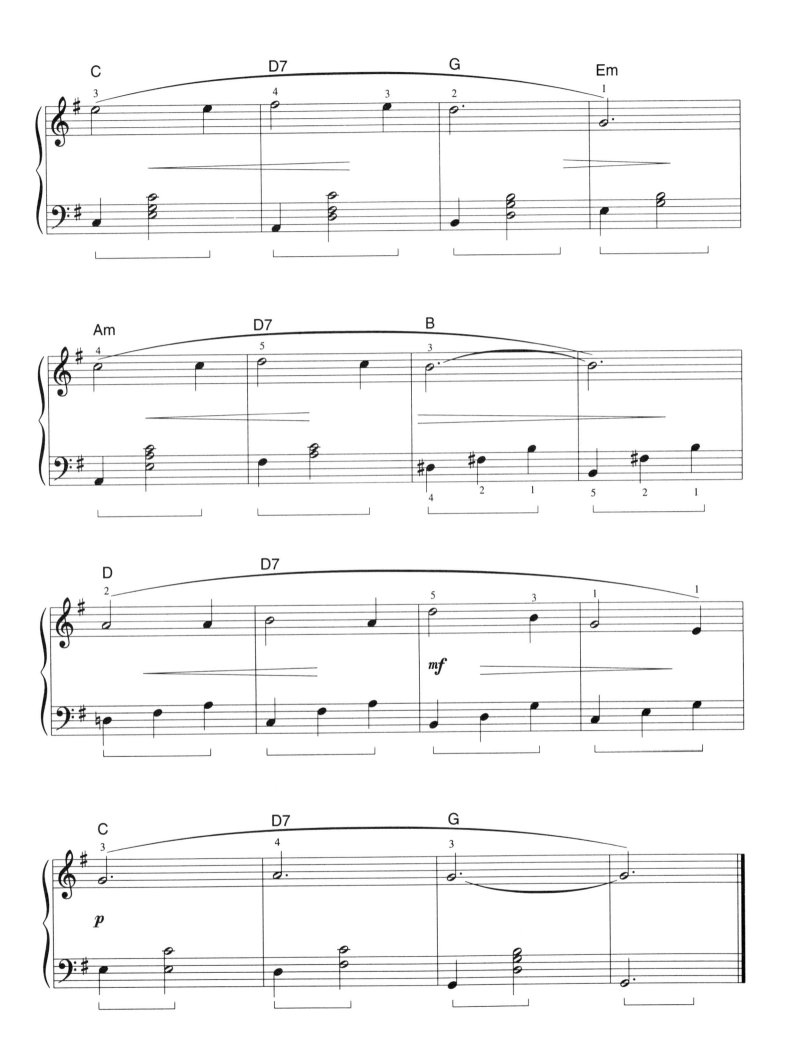

MILITARY POLONAISE
Op.40 No. 1

Frederic Chopin

D.C. al Fine

MINUET IN G

Johann Sebastian Bach

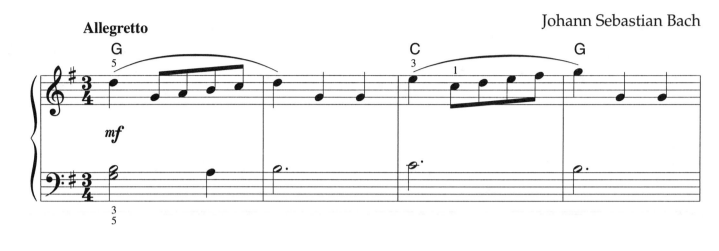

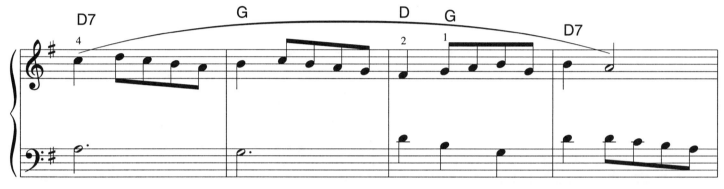

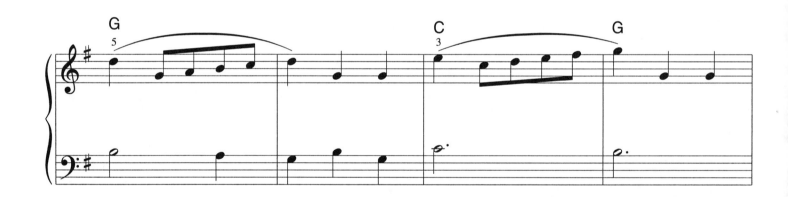

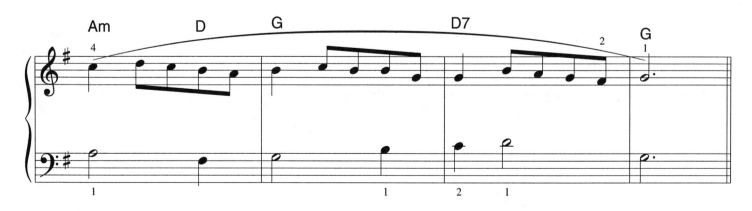

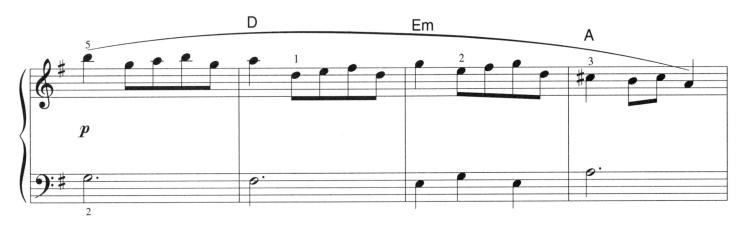

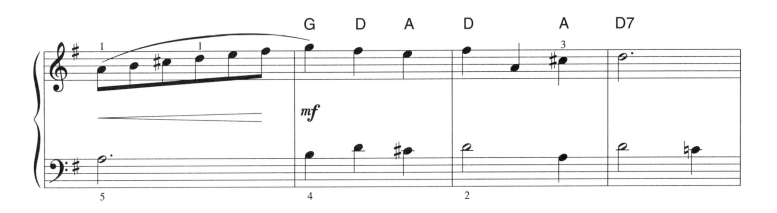

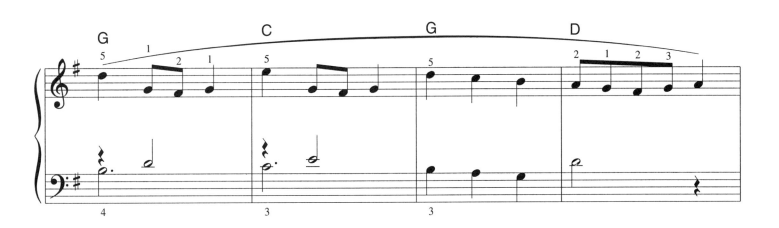

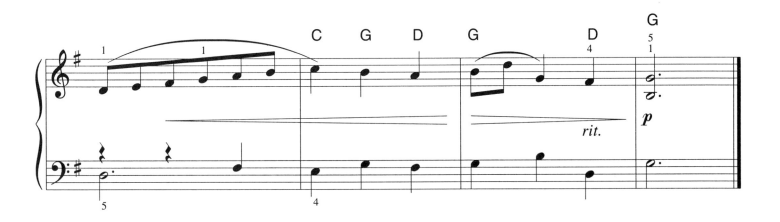

A NIGHT ON BALD MOUNTAIN

Modest Mussorgsky

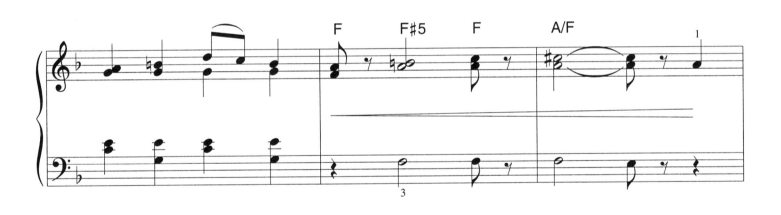

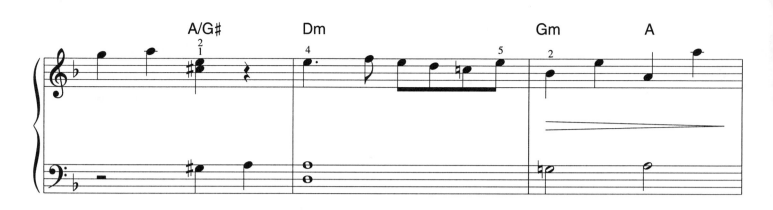

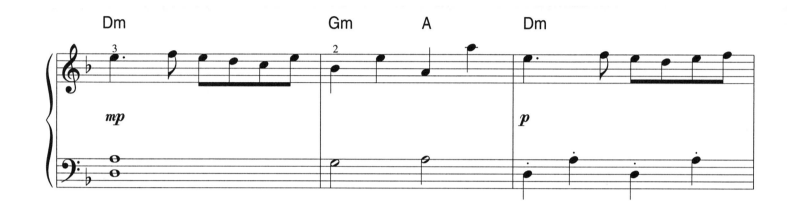

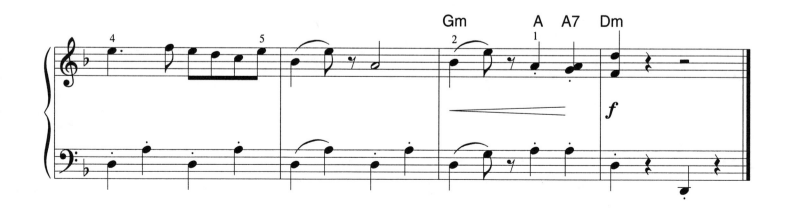

MY HEART EVER FAITHFUL
(Cantata No. 68)

Johann Sebastian Bach

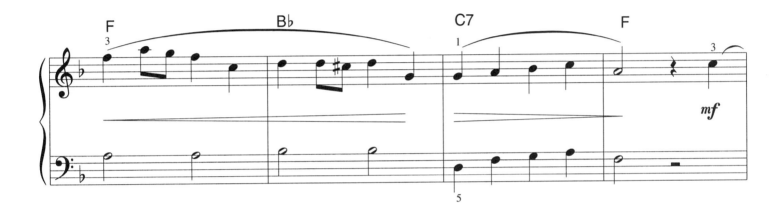

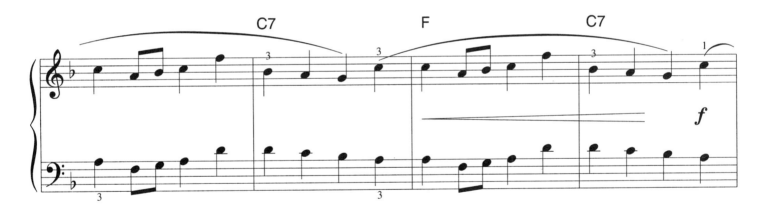

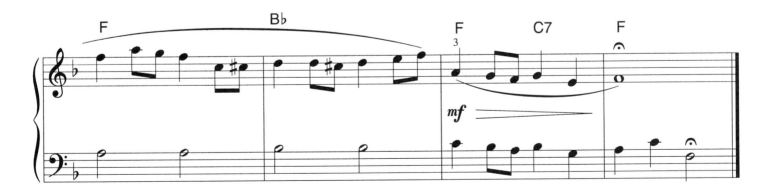

NONE BUT THE LONELY HEART

Expressively, but not dragging

Pyotr Ilyich Tchaikovsky

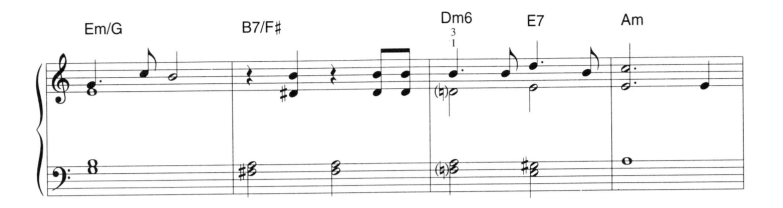

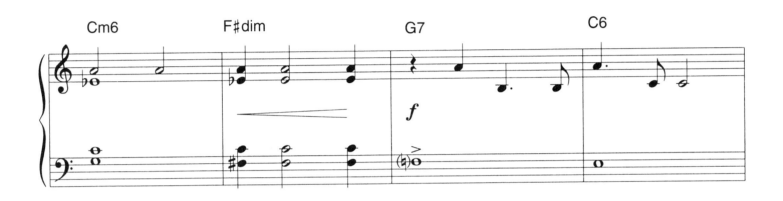

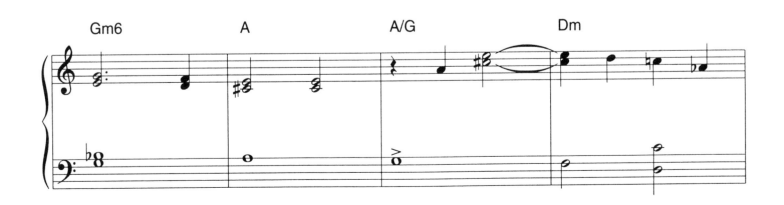

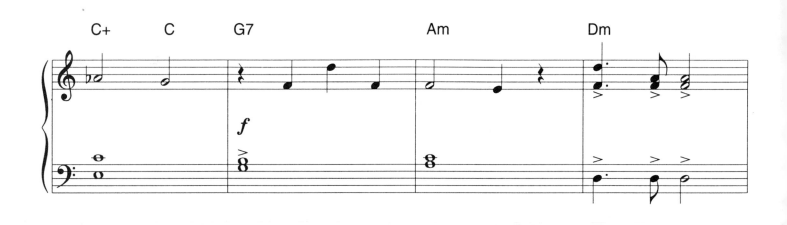

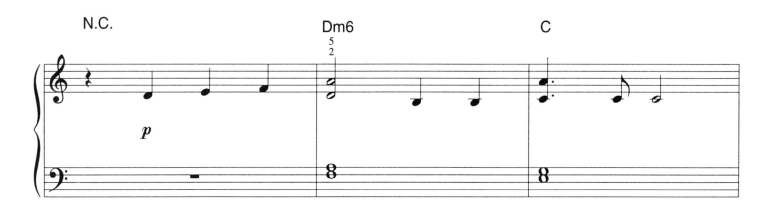

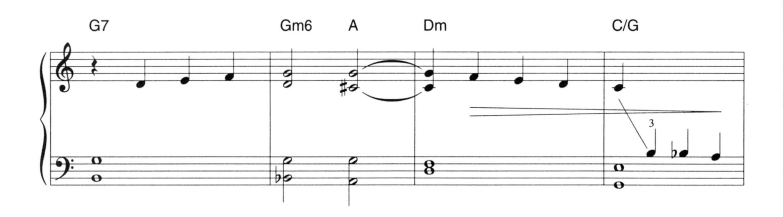

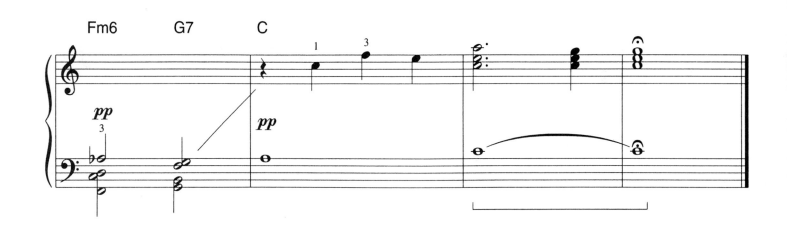

THE PASTORAL THEME
(from Symphony No. 6)

Ludwig van Beethoven

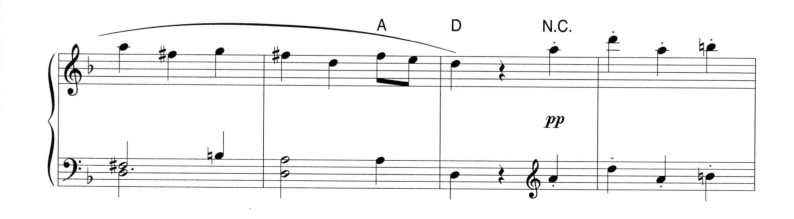

PEASANT DANCE
(Opus 39)

Dmitri Kabalevsky

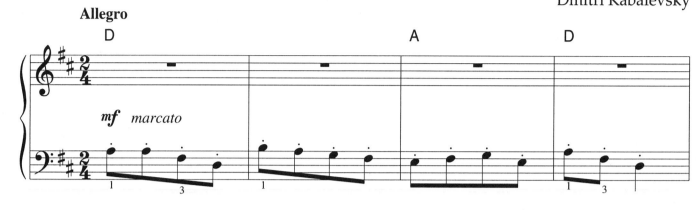

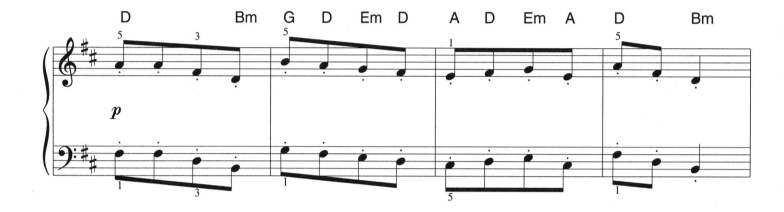

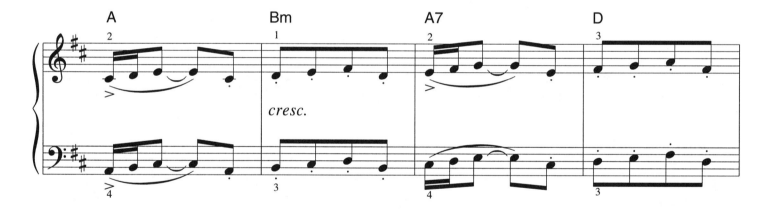

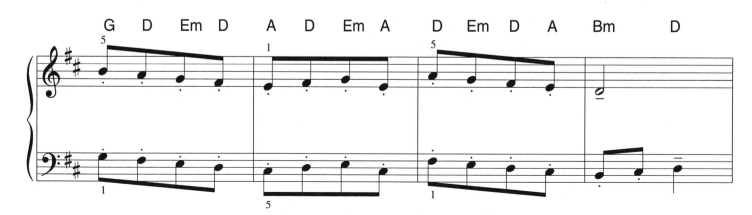

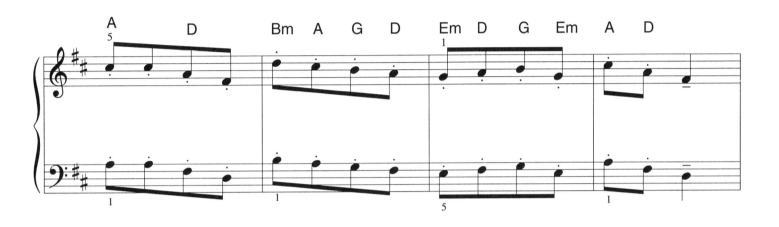

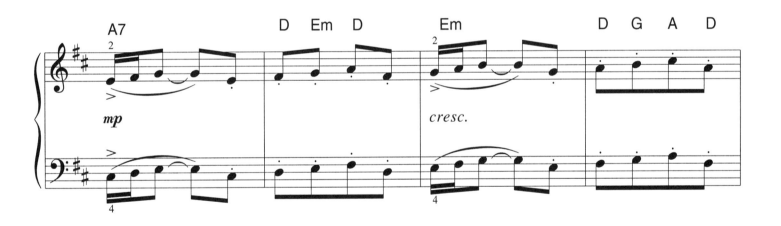

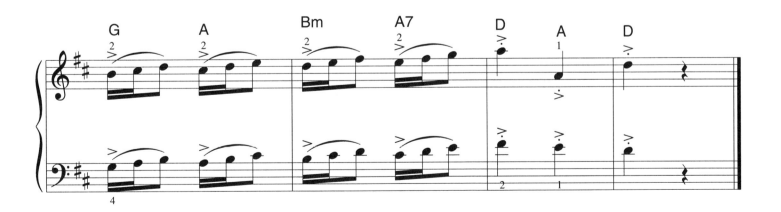

Theme from
PETER AND THE WOLF

Serge Prokofiev

Lively, gaily

Theme from
PIANO CONCERTO NO. 1 IN C
(Rondo)

Ludwig van Beethoven

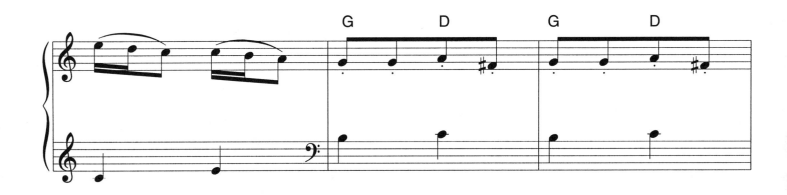

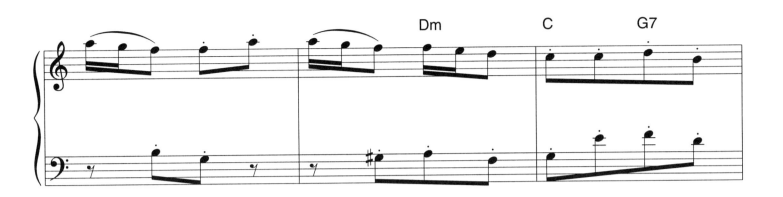

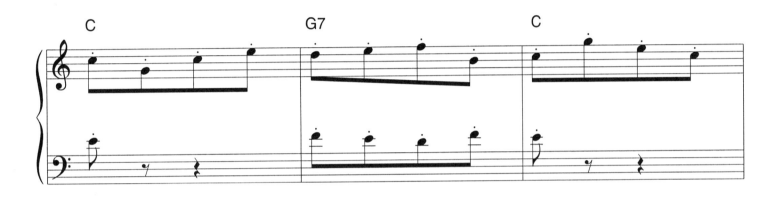

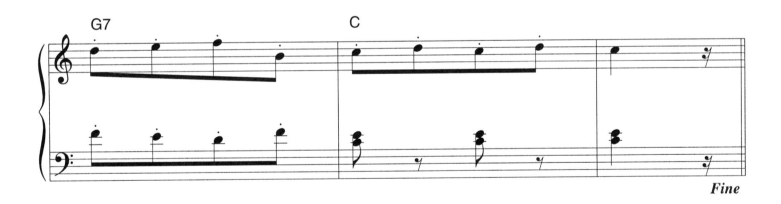

Fine

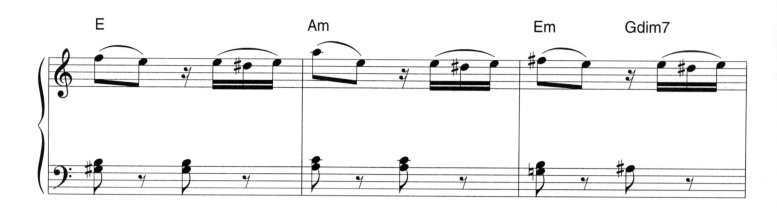

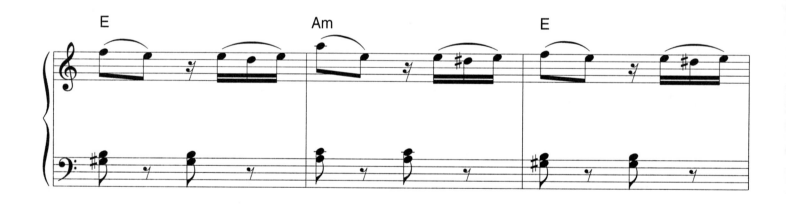

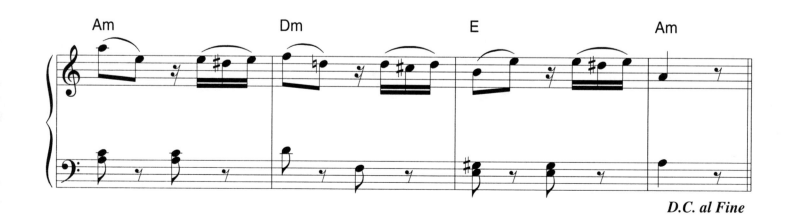

D.C. al Fine

Theme from
PIANO SONATA
(Opus 26)

Ludwig van Beethoven

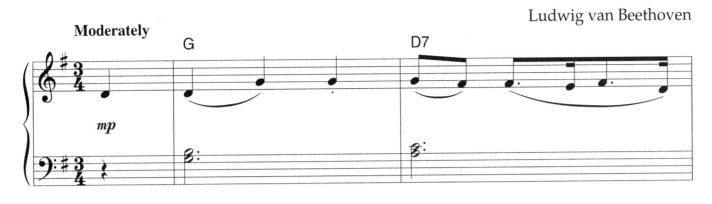

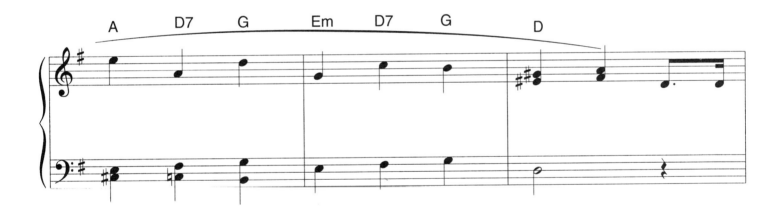

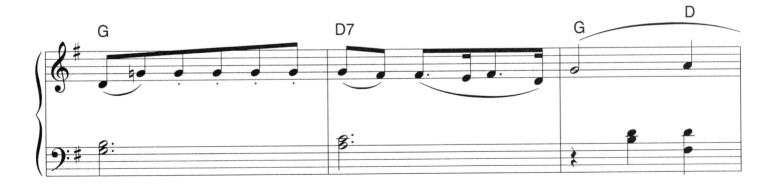

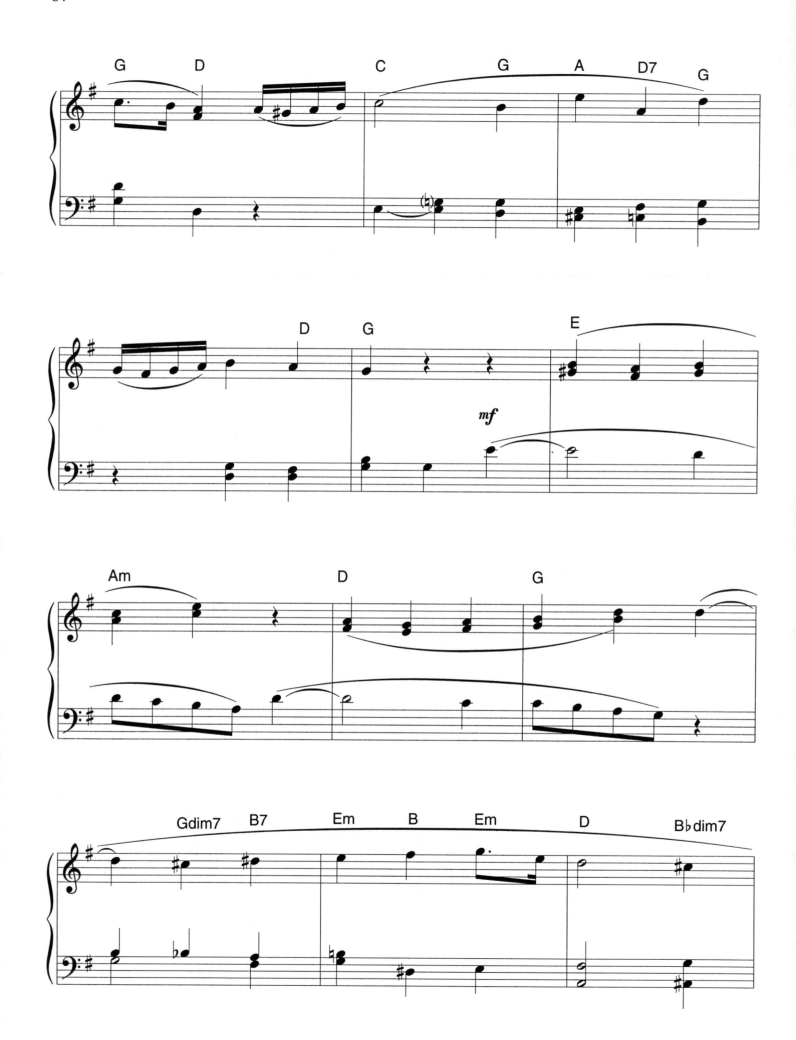

84

Theme from
PIANO SONATA
(Opus 90)

Ludwig van Beethoven

87

PLAISIR D'AMOUR

G. P. Martini

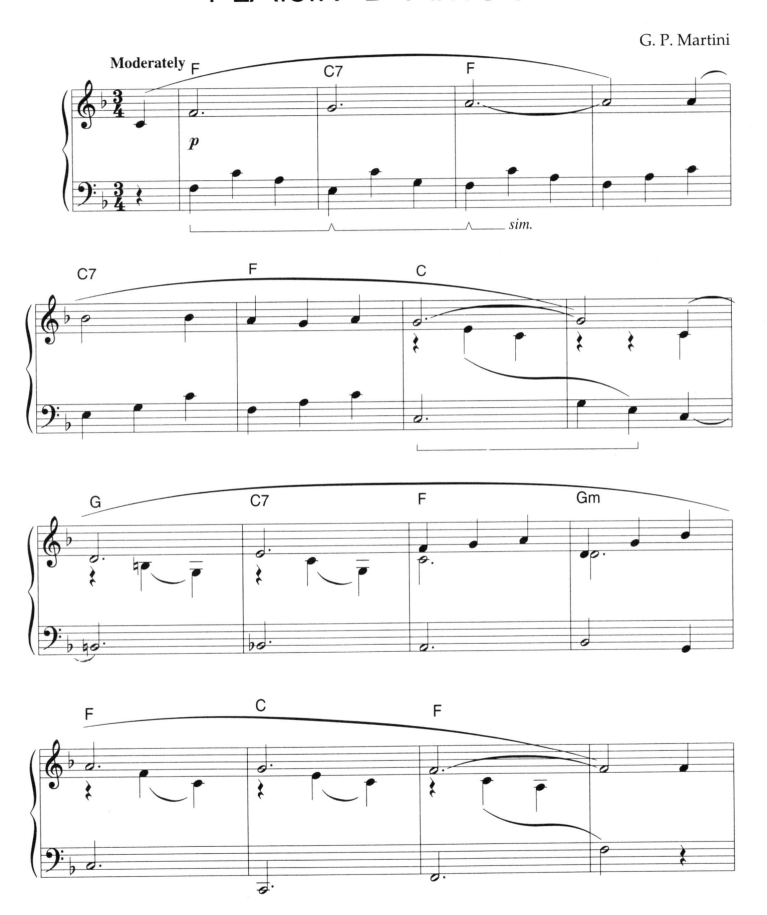

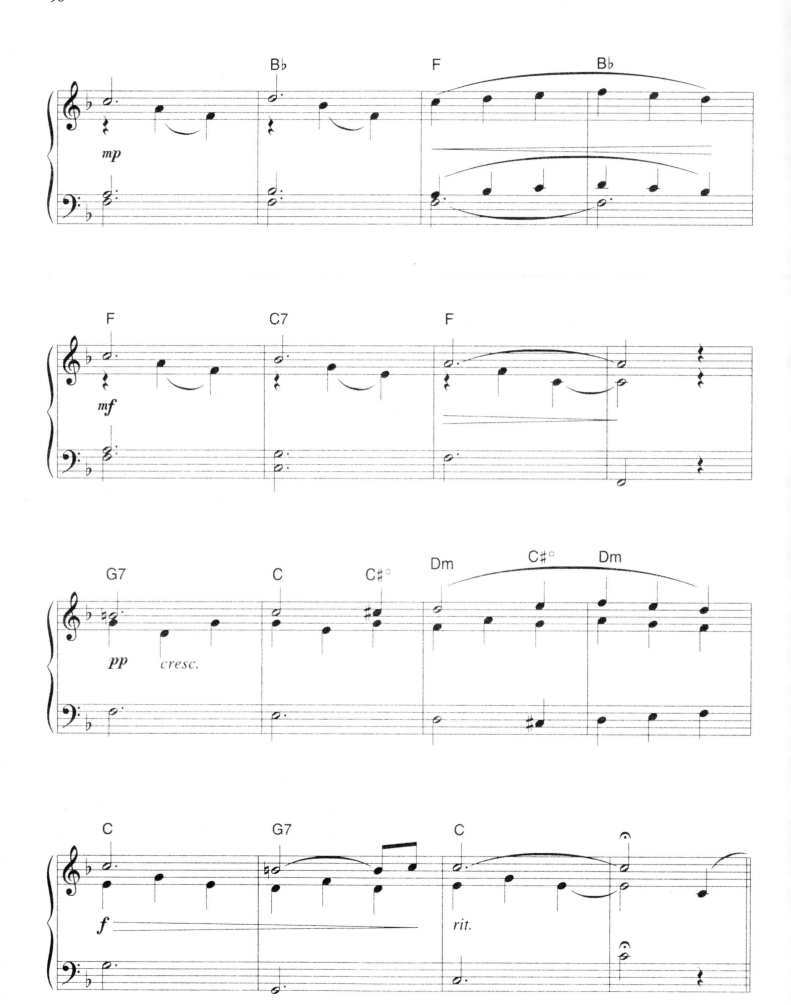

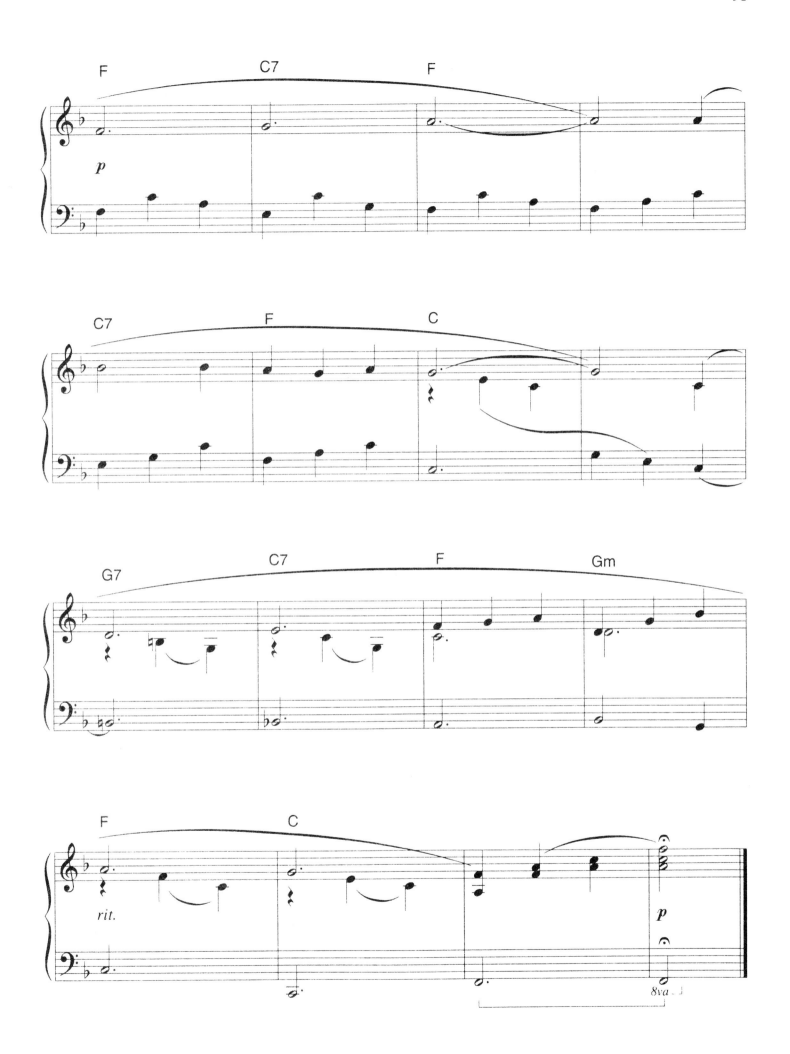

Theme from
PIANO TRIO NO. 2

Franz Schubert

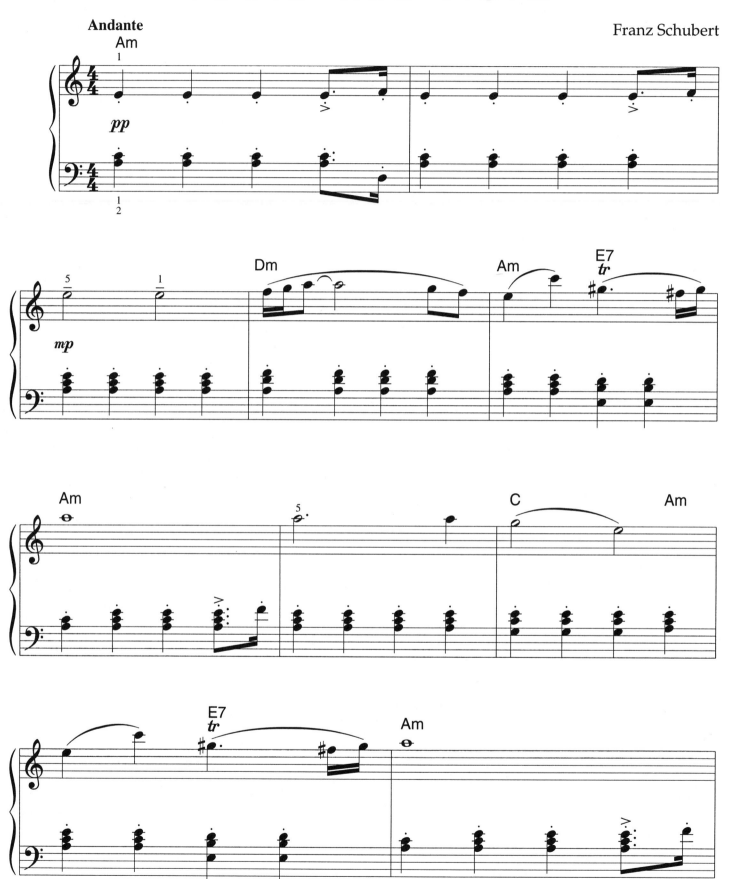

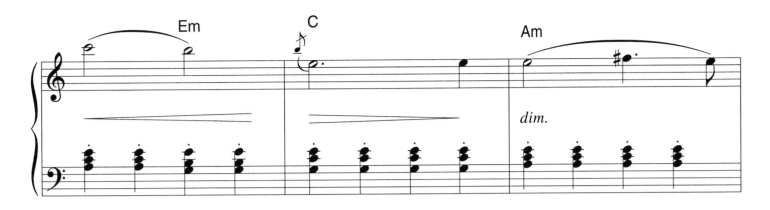

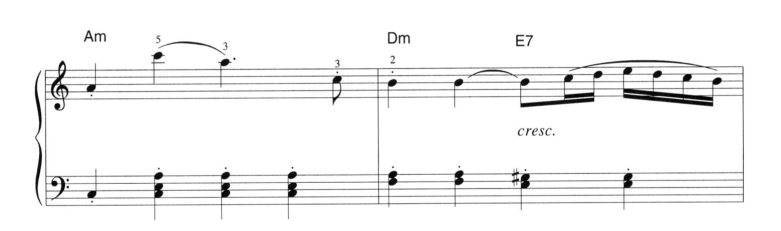

POLKA FROM "ORPHEUS"

Jacques Offenbach

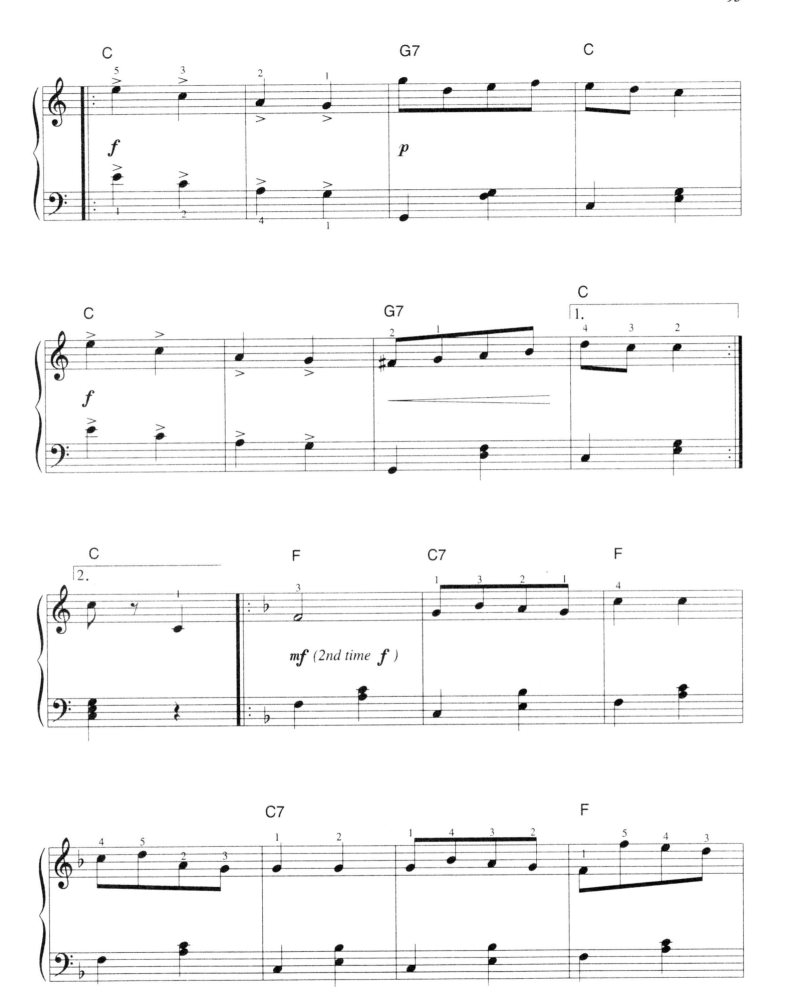

POMP AND CIRCUMSTANCE

Edward Elgar

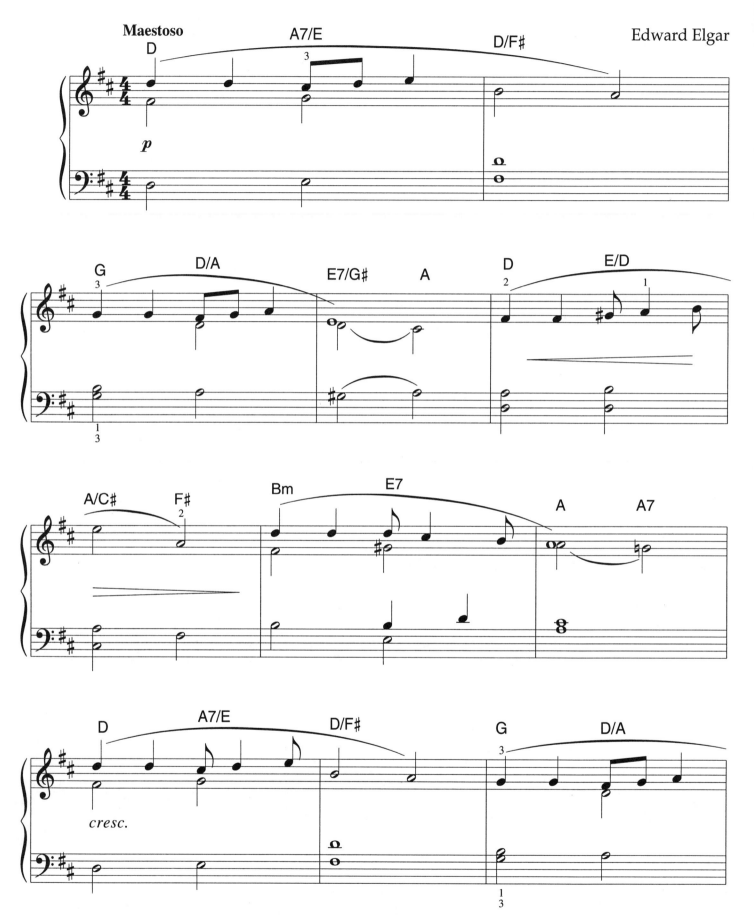

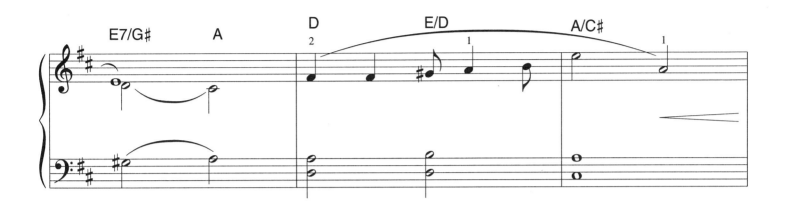

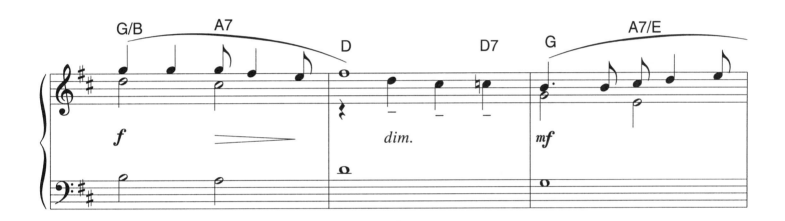

THE ROCKING HORSE
(Opus 63)

Moderato

Louis Streabbog

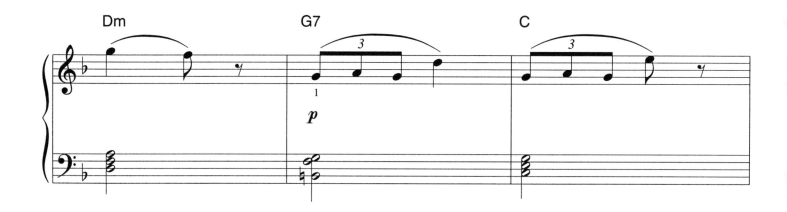

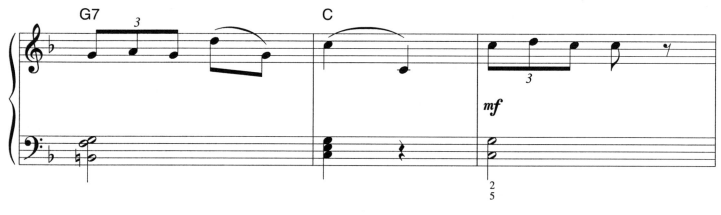

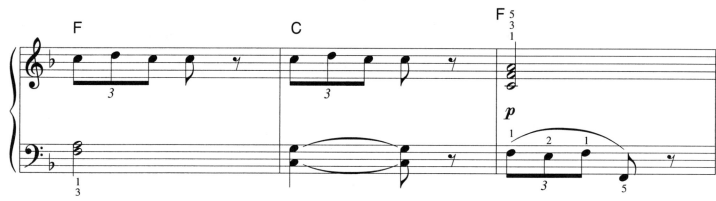

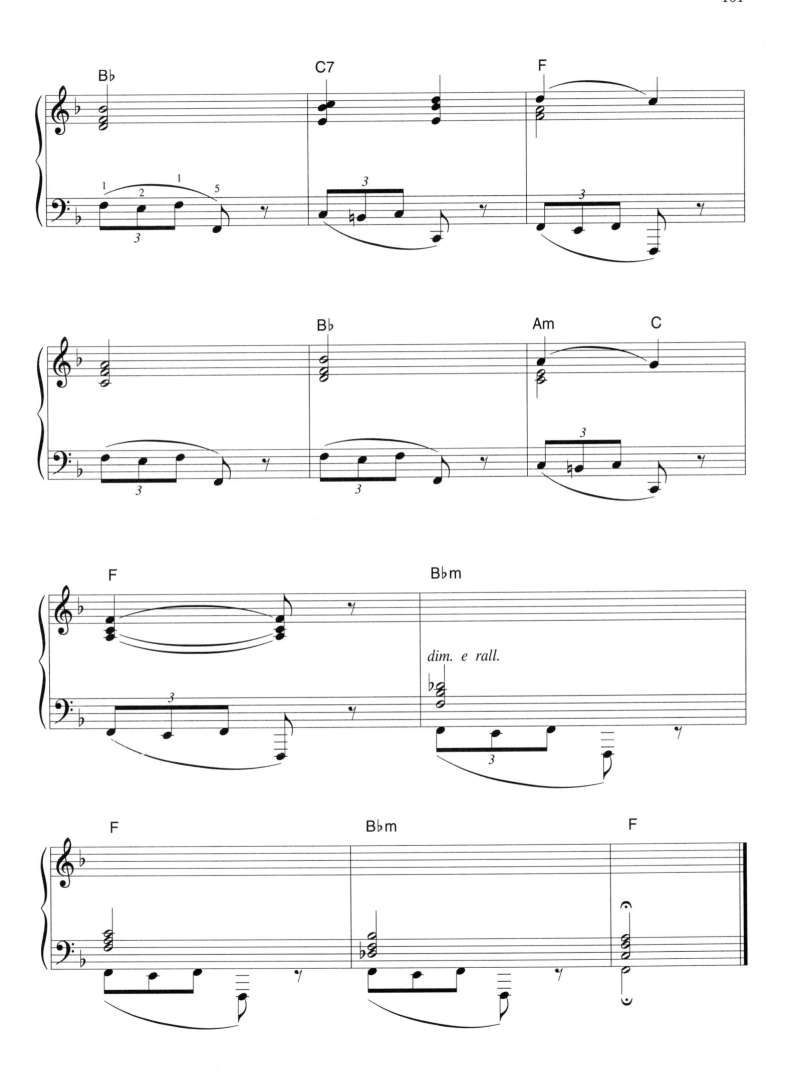

ROMANCE
(FROM EINE KLEINE NACHTMUSIK)

Wolfgang Amadeus Mozart

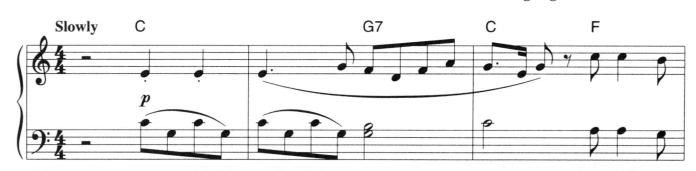

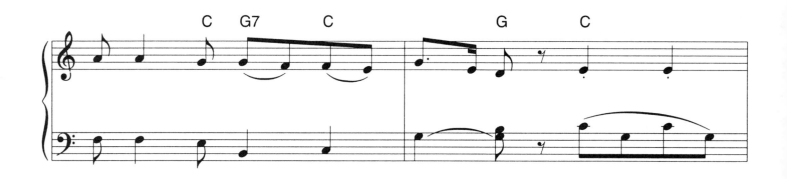

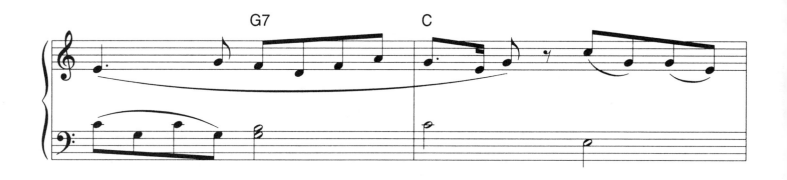

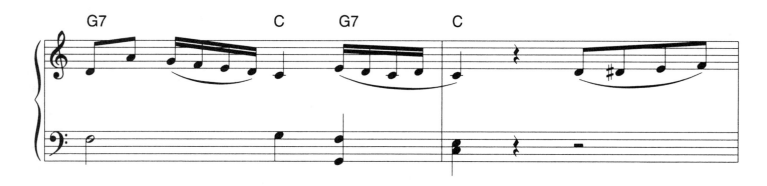

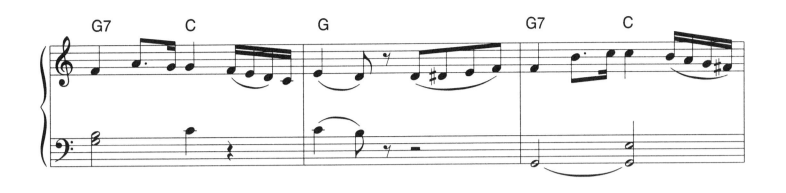

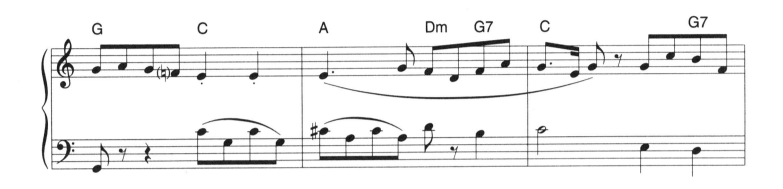

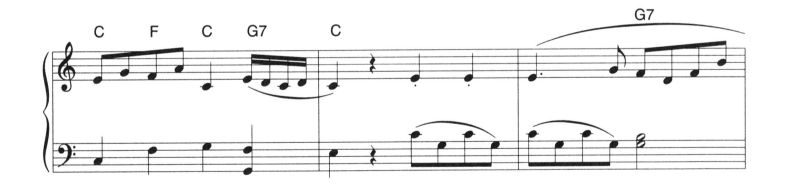

ROMANCE IN F

Ludwig van Beethoven

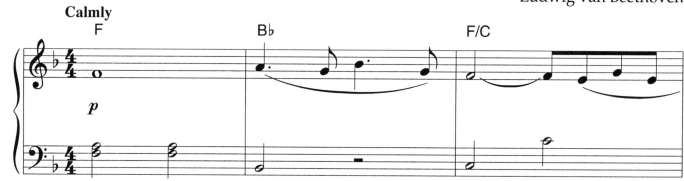

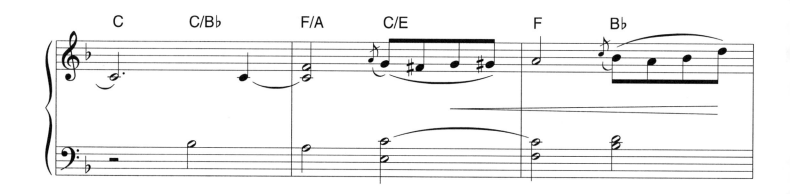

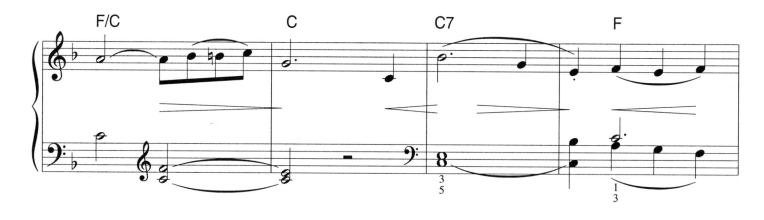

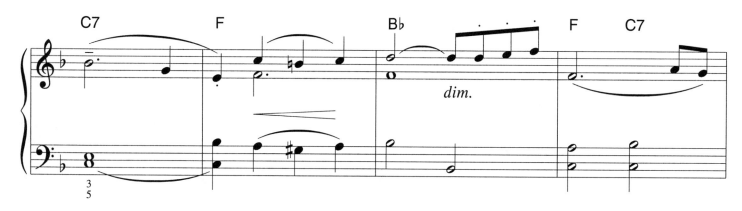

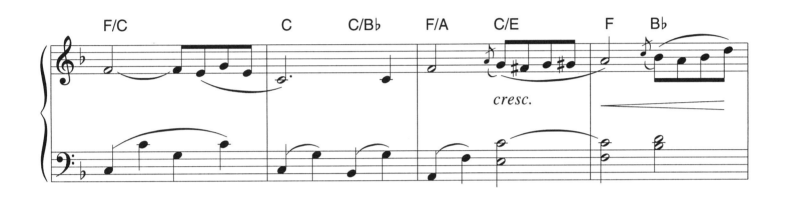

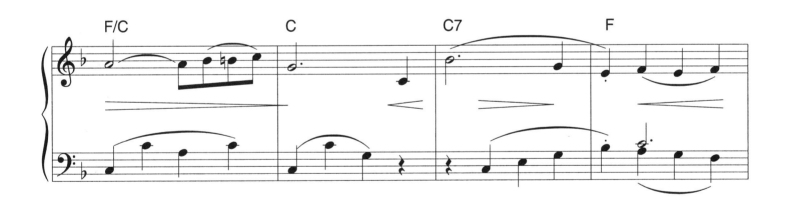

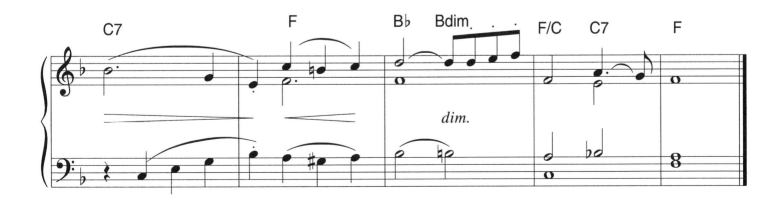

RONDO ALLA TURCA
(FROM SONATA IN A)

Wolfgang Amadeus Mozart

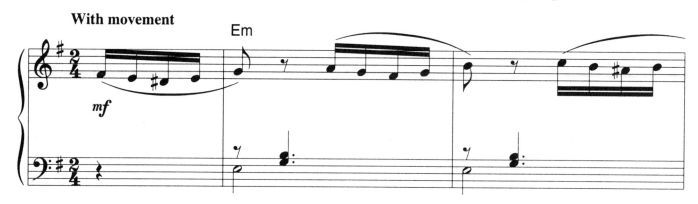

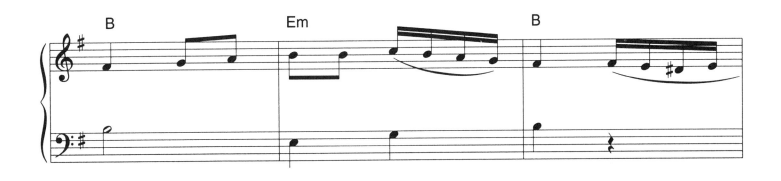

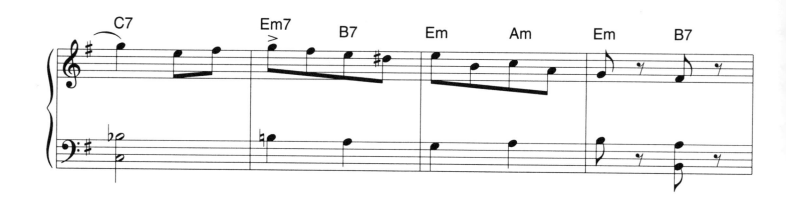

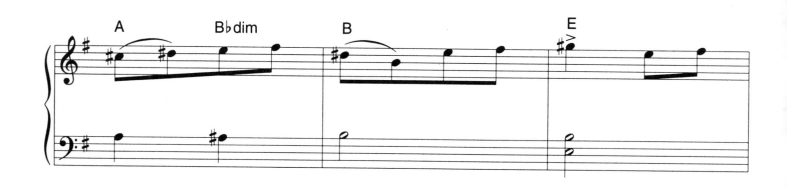

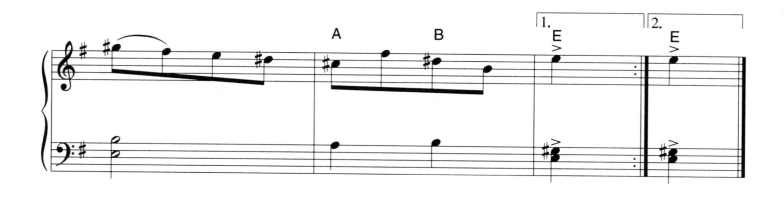

SCARBOROUGH FAIR

English

SABRE DANCE
FROM "GAYNE BALLET"

Aram Khachaturian

SCHEHEREZADE
(Theme)

Nicolai Rimsky-Korsakoff

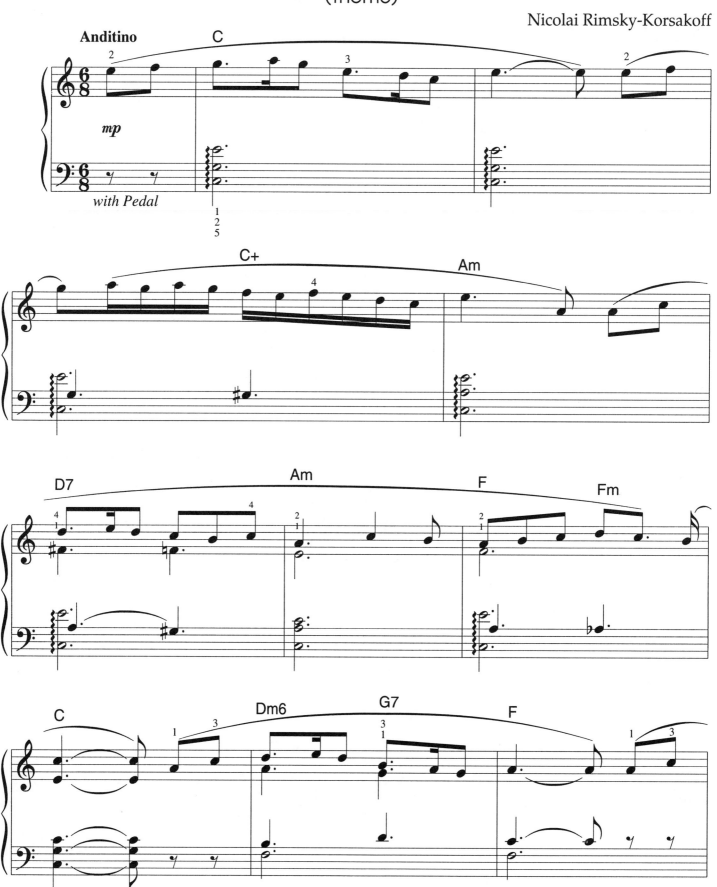

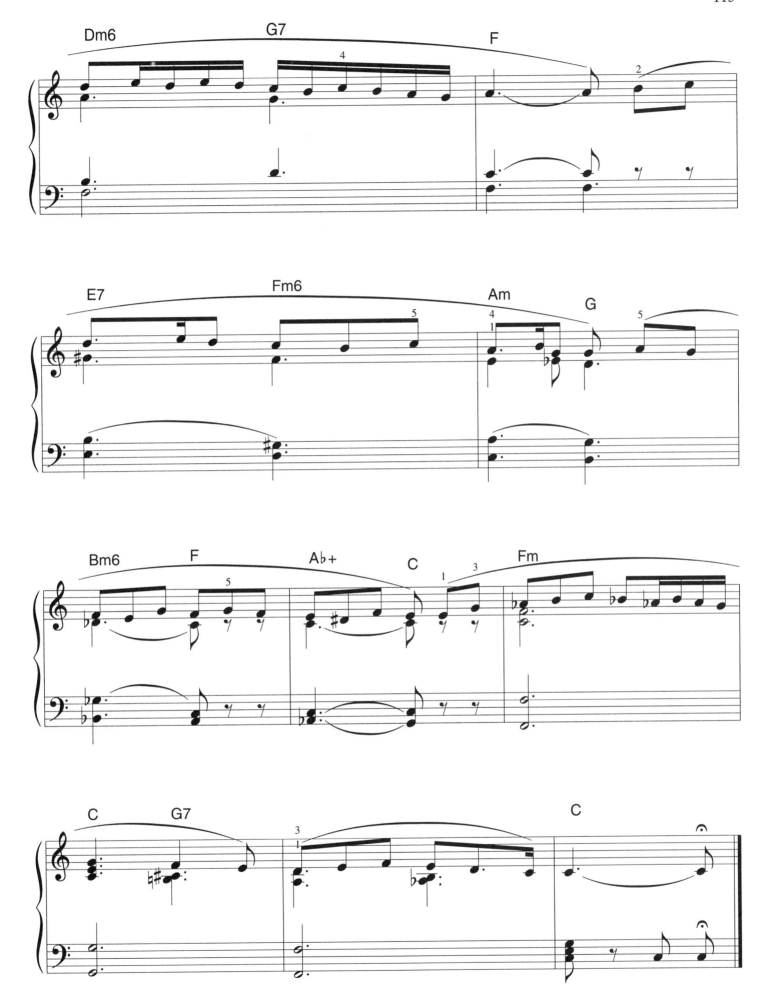

SPRING SONG

Allegretto grazioso

Felix Mendelssohn

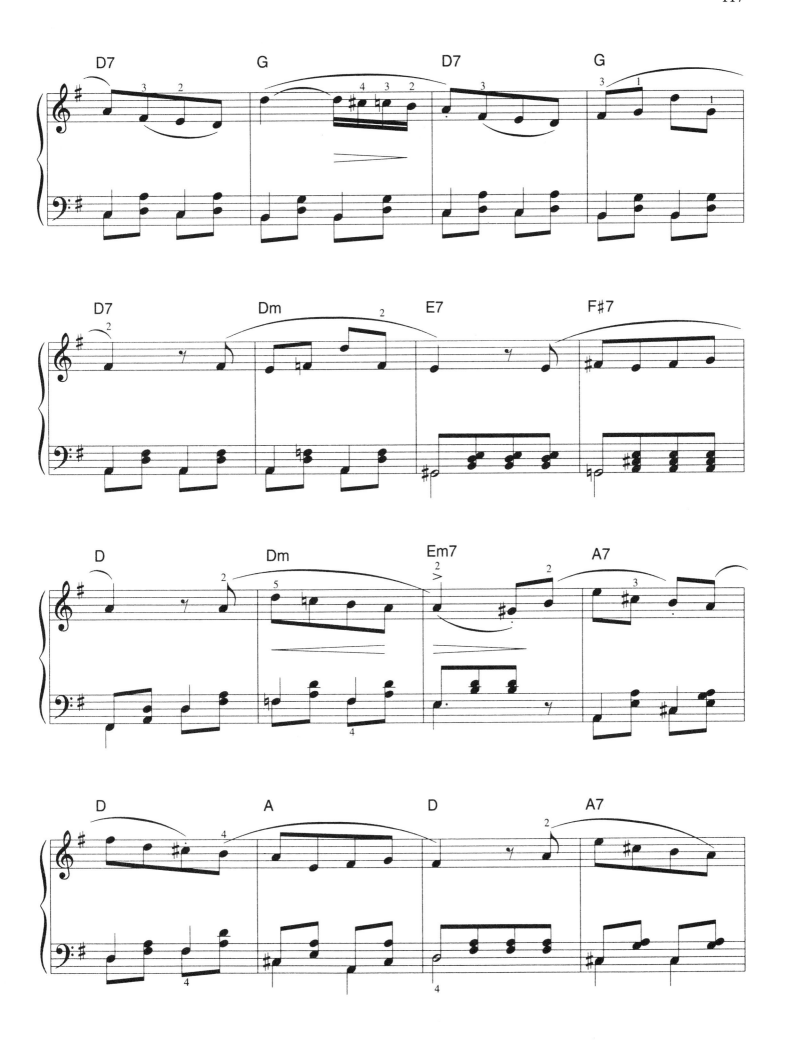

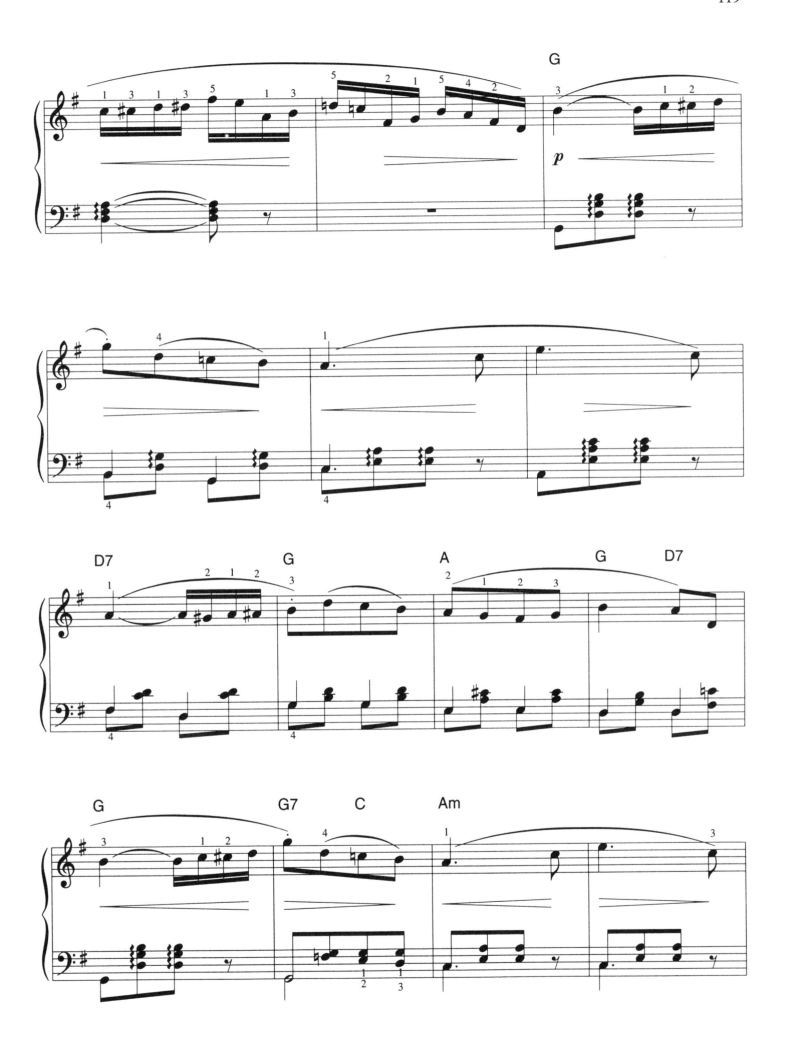

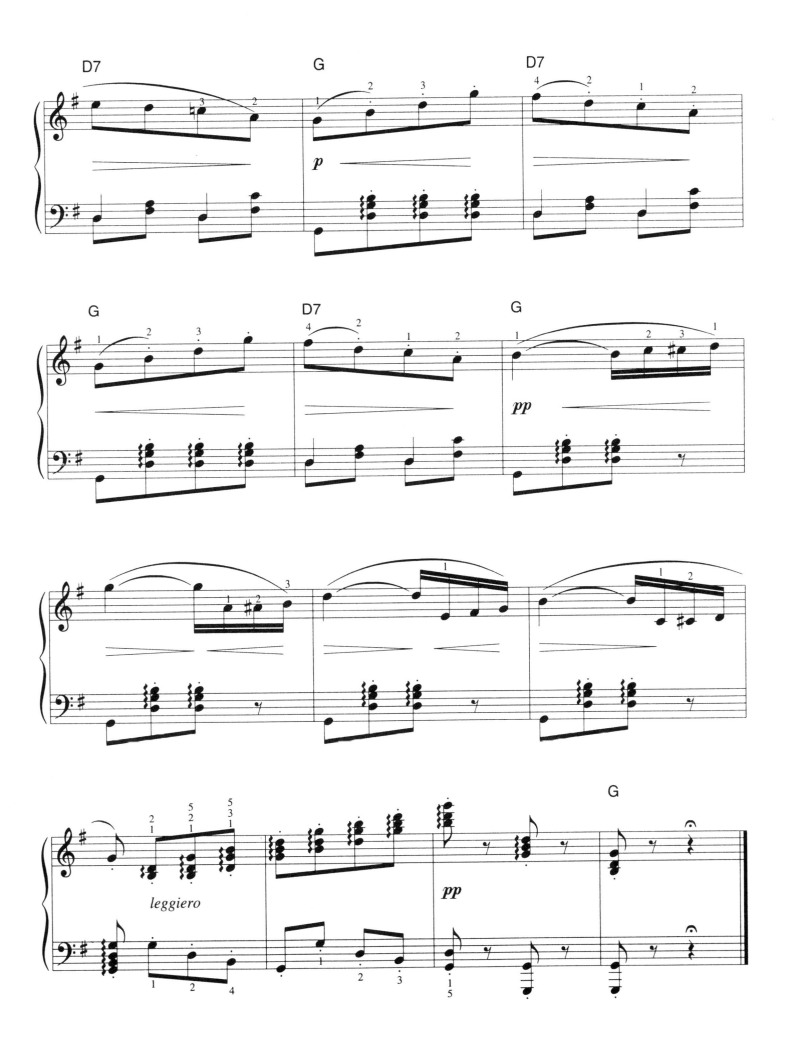

122

Theme from
"ST. ANTHONY" VARIATIONS

Johannes Brahms

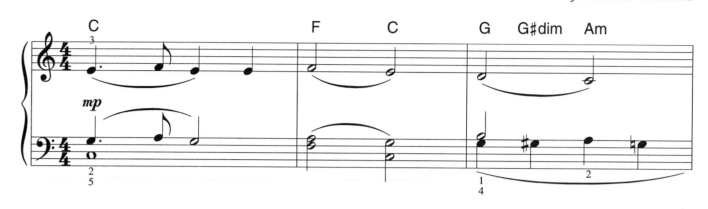

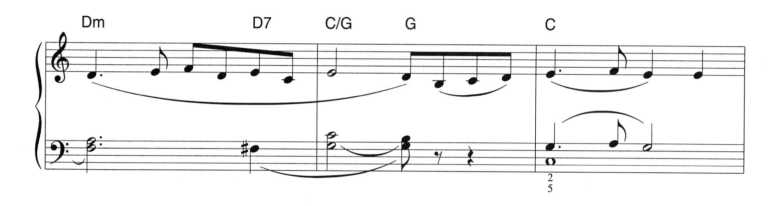

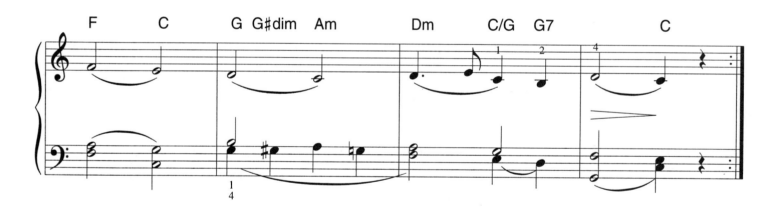

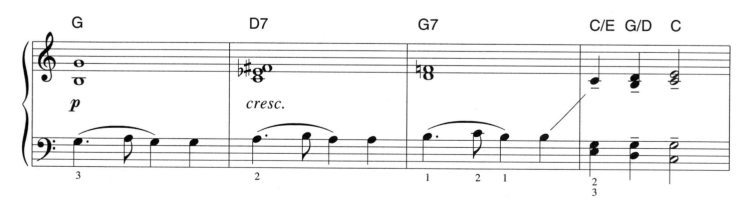

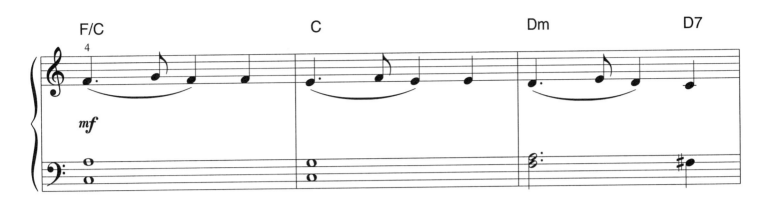

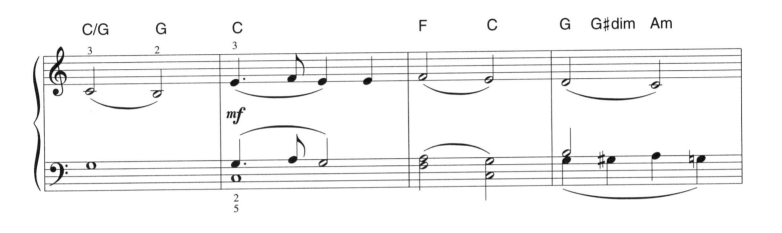

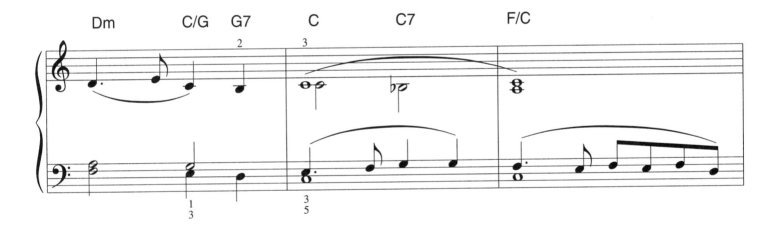

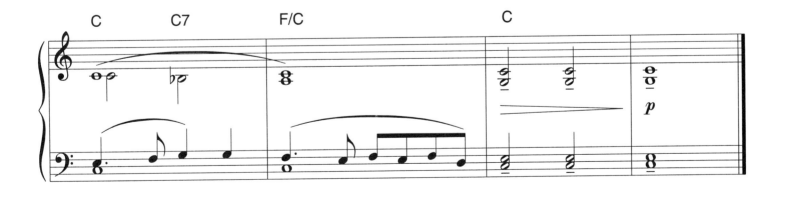

SUNDAY IN THE PARK

Moderato (con spritito)

Muzio Clementi

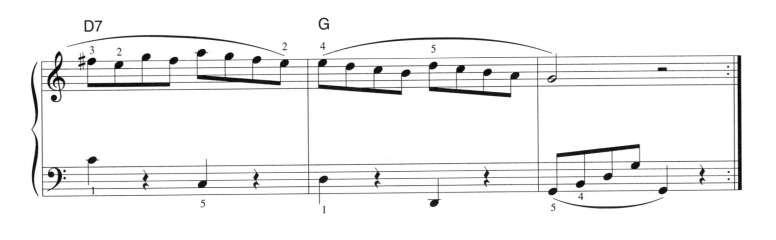

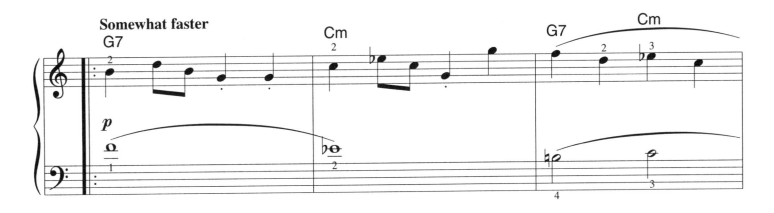

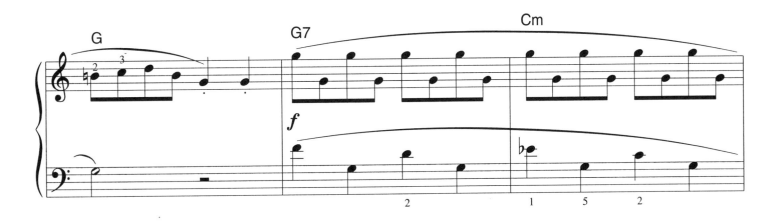

TOCCATINA
(Opus 27)

Dmitri Kabalevsky

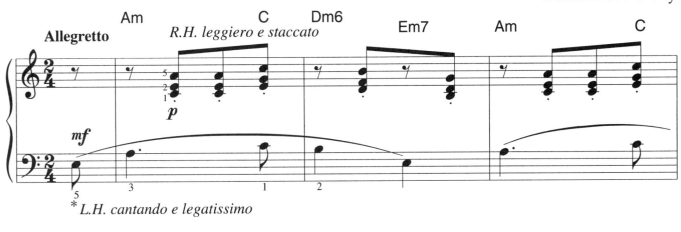

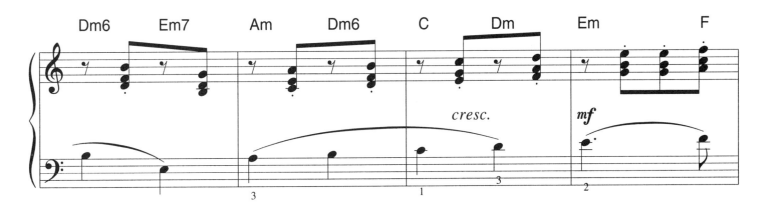

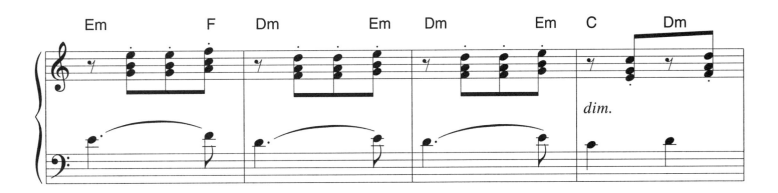

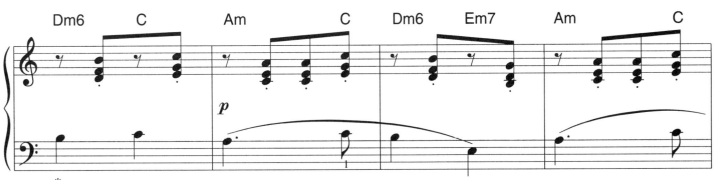

* Senza Pedale

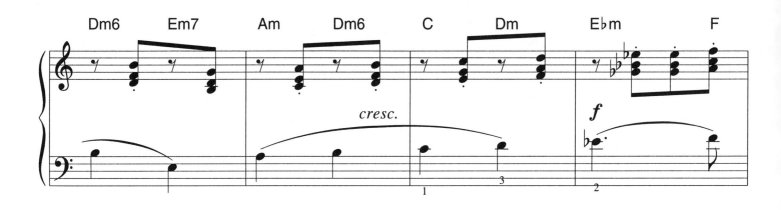

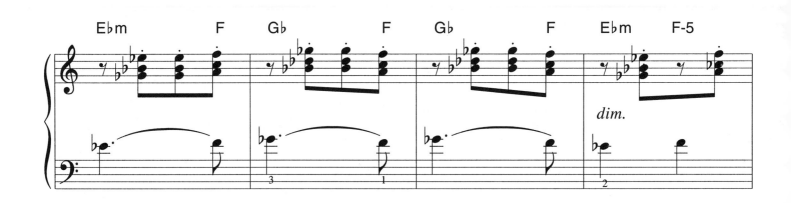

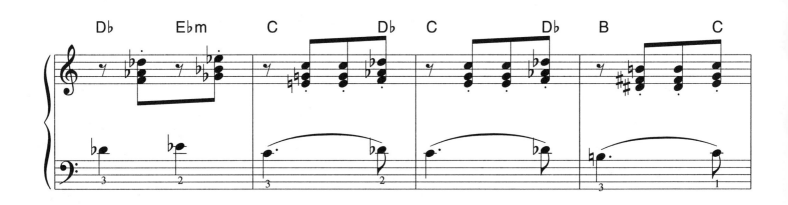

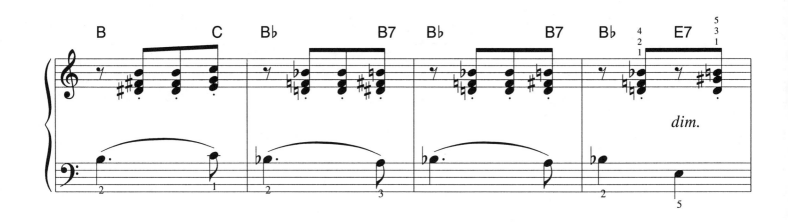

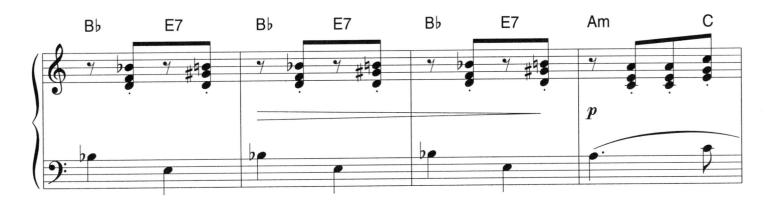

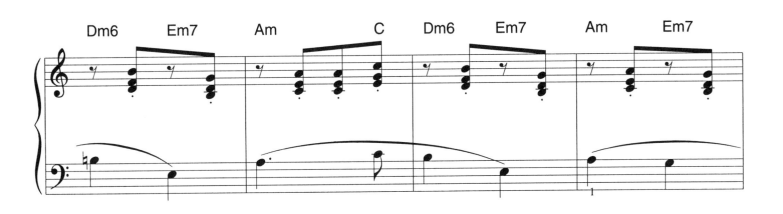

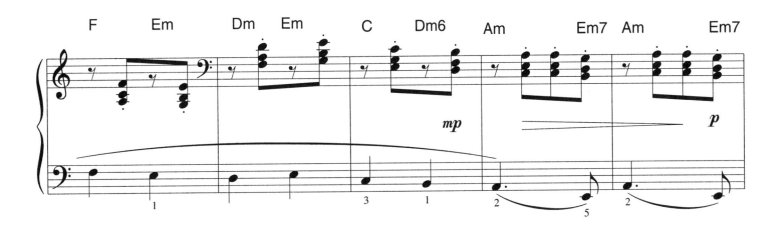

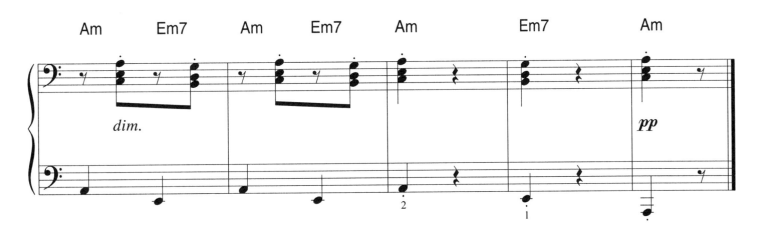

Theme from
SYMPHONY NO. 7

Ludwig van Beethoven

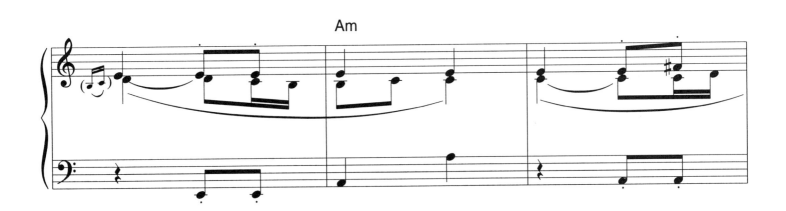

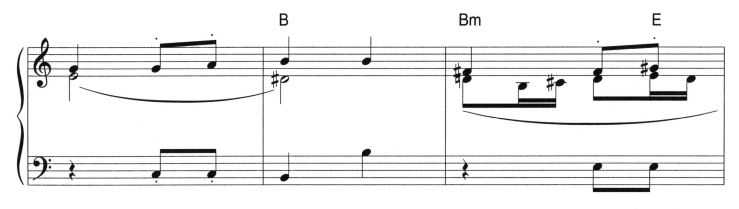

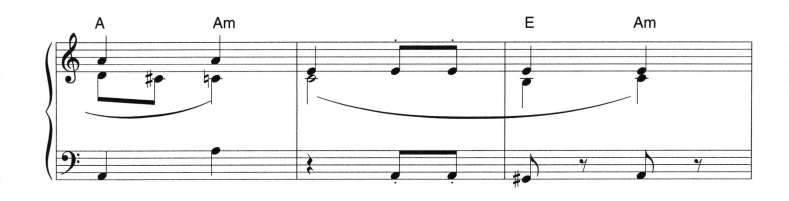

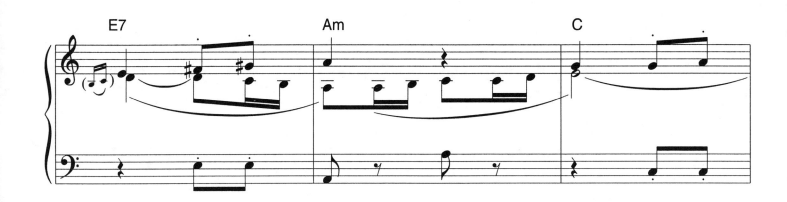

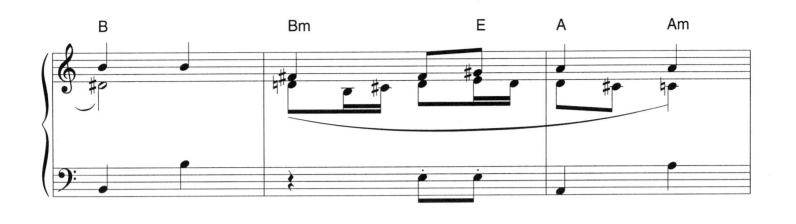

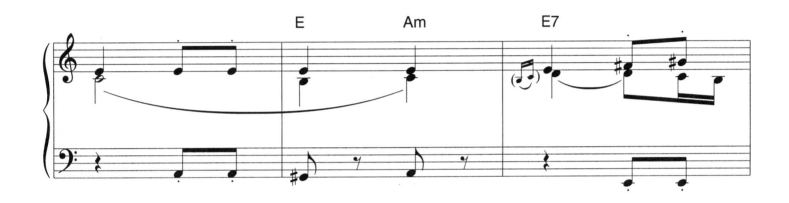

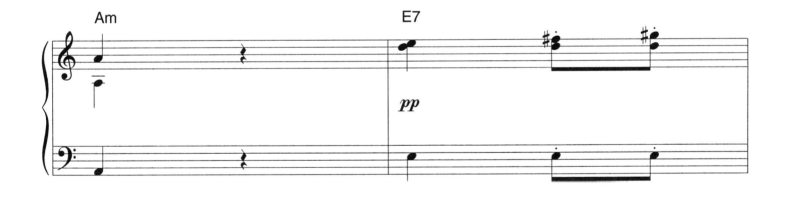

TOPSY TURVY

Cornelius Gurlitt

Moderato

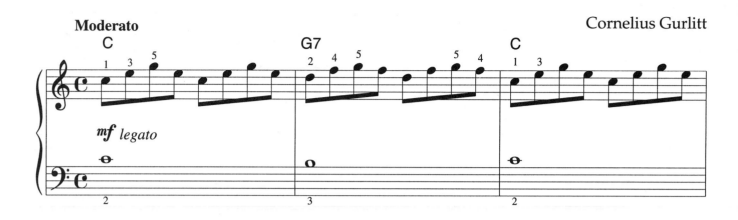

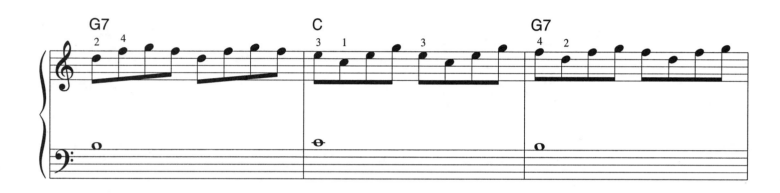

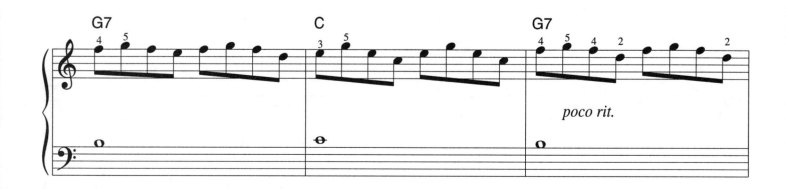

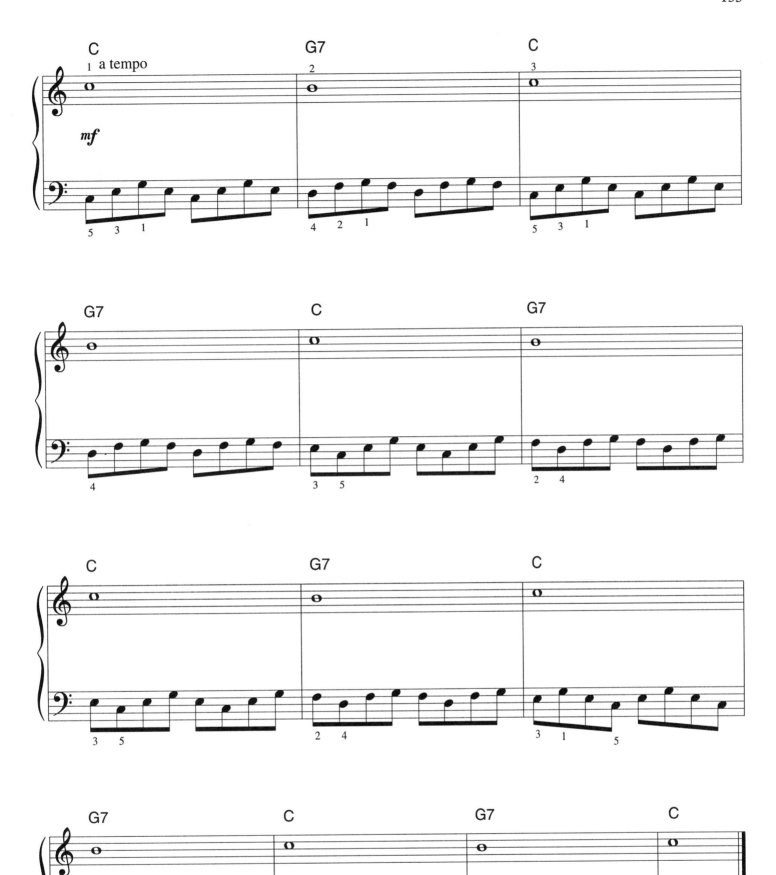

Theme from
VIOLIN CONCERTO

Johannes Brahms

YOU'LL LAY YOUR HAND IN MINE
(FROM DON GIOVANNI)

Wolfgang Amadeus Mozart

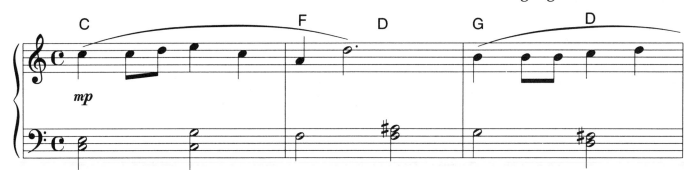

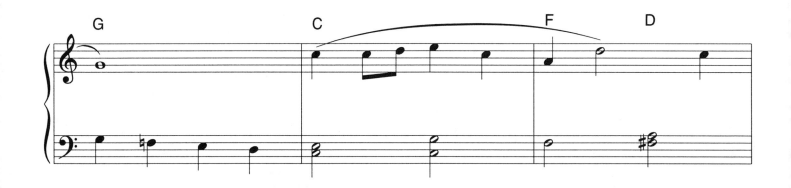

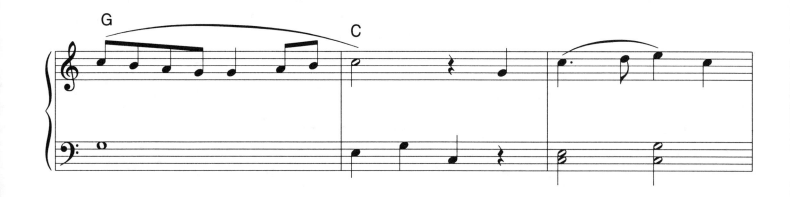

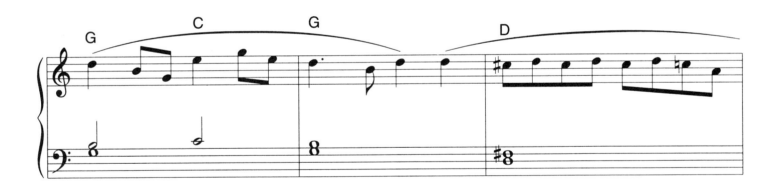

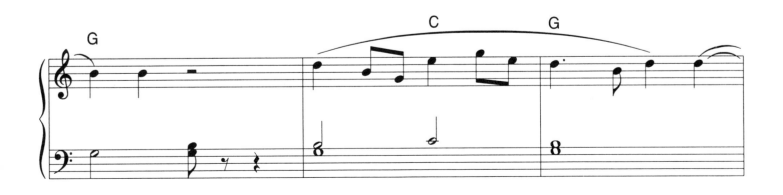

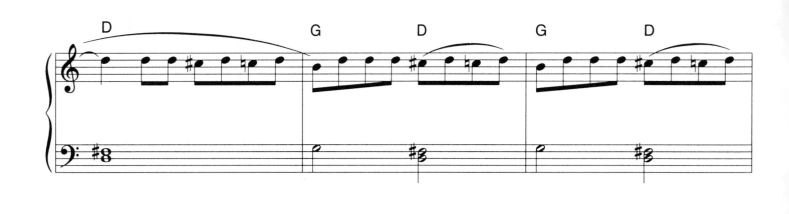

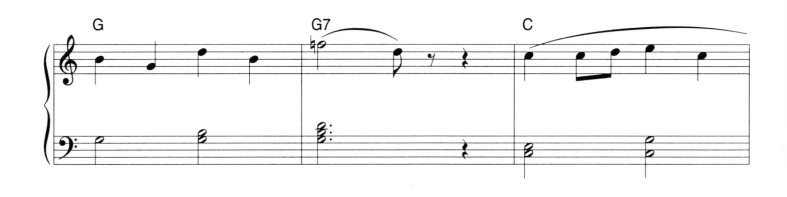

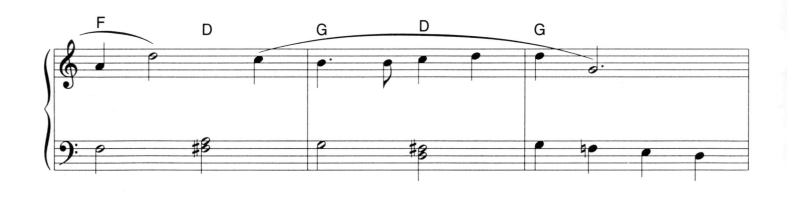

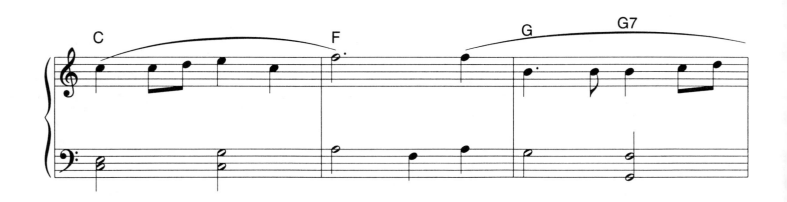

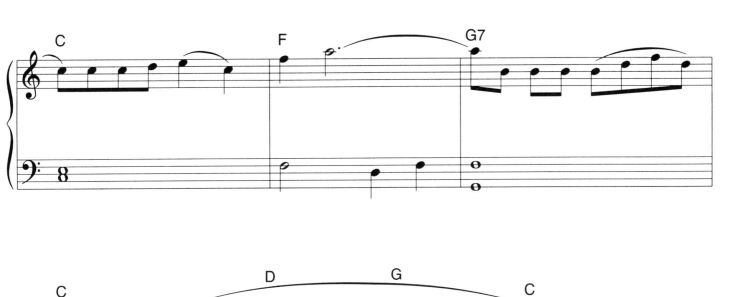

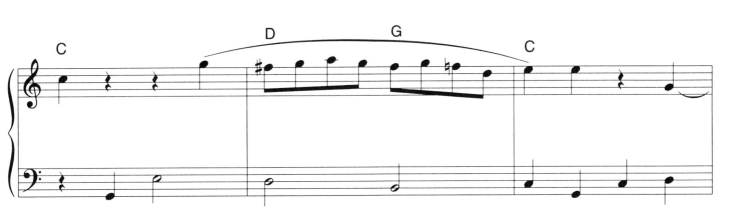

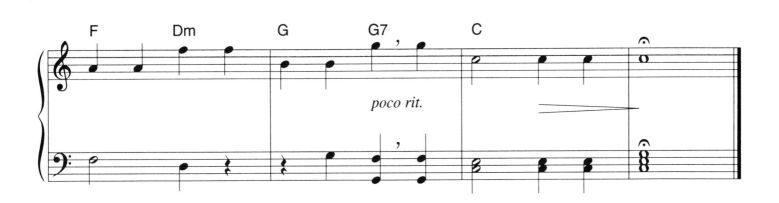

poco rit.

YOU CAN'T EVADE THE TRUTH
(from "Carmen")

Georges Bizet

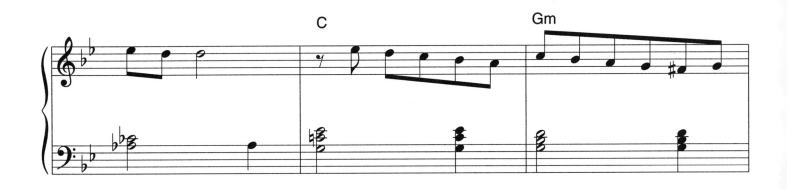

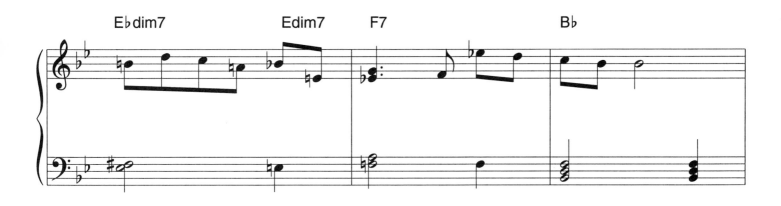

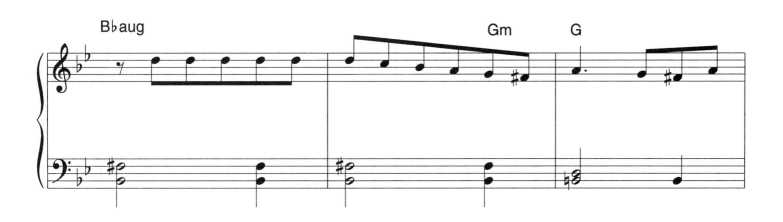

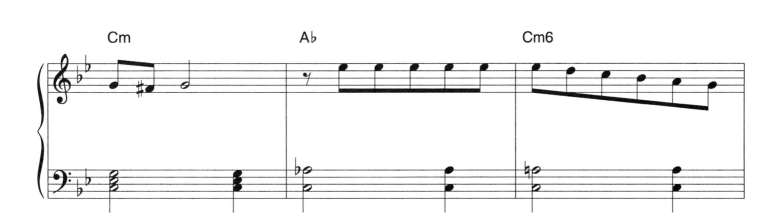

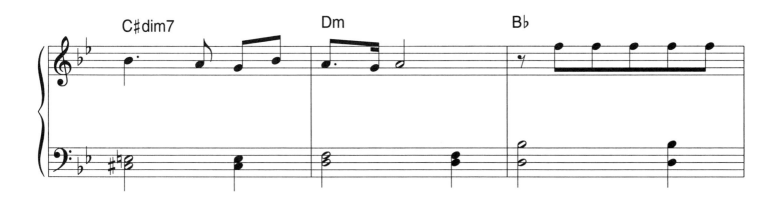

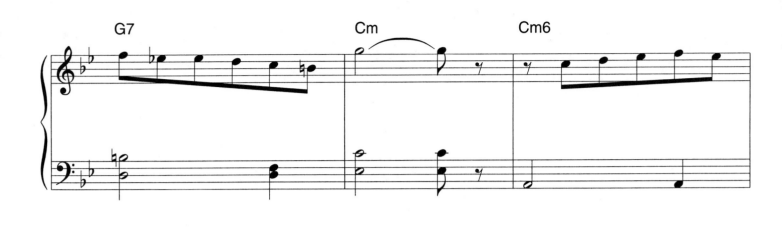

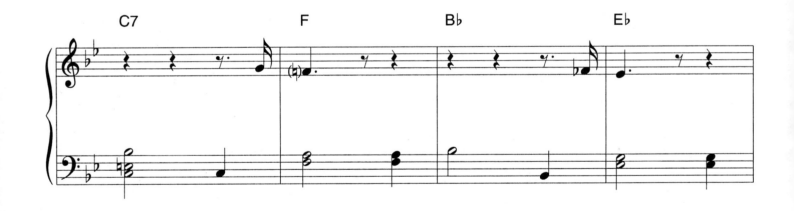

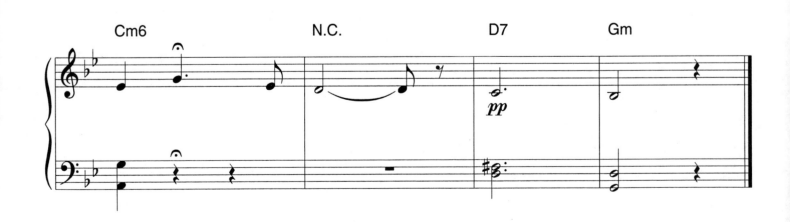